ULTIMATE
CHINA
GUIDE

ULTIMATE CHINA GUIDE

**How to Teach English, Travel,
Learn Chinese & Find Work in China**

NICK LENCZEWSKI
(LEN-CHESS-KEY)

ISBN: 978-1-5303-3262-5

Ultimate China Guide
Minneapolis, Minnesota 55422
www.ultimatechinaguide.com

nick@ultimatechinaguide.com
651-795-9483

TABLE OF CONTENTS

CHAPTER 1

INTRODUCTION
An Alternative Career Path

"Not all those who wander are lost."
—JRR TOLKIEN, *The Lord of the Rings*

"WHAT ARE SOME OF your career goals?" the interviewer asked me.

A job fair for soon-to-be college graduates in Minnesota was held each February and my friends and I had driven into the city to be a part of it. We didn't have any ideas about what to do with our lives after college, so we figured we might as well check it out.

"To not have to work?" I thought. Wasn't this everyone's honest career goal when they were 22? This is what I really wanted to say, for who would want to get up every morning, commute to an office, stress out every day, and watch TV at night in order to unwind if they didn't have to?

1

"I studied math in college because I've been drawn to numbers all my life and a business analyst is something I've always seen myself wanting to be," I answered instead. The financial services company interviewer smiled and nodded, taking down notes. I was sure he had heard the same answer before and deep inside, like me, he knew the question he had asked reveals little about a person's ambitions.

"Thank you for your time today, we'll be getting back to you," he said as he shook my hand.

At 22, it was obvious to me that I didn't want a job at this point in my life. As far as I could tell, I would mainly be drinking coffee and staring at Excel documents. When I was a kid, it was school that was always in the way of learning and doing interesting things: exploring the town I lived in via bike and canoe; learning to play Beethoven and Scott Joplin on piano; playing hockey with my friends without a coach making it too competitive to be enjoyed; reading JRR Tolkien and Terry Brooks fantasy stories and then writing my own tales; traveling to other countries. A job seemed like school for adults and upon graduating from college, 40 more years of it with only one or two vacations a year wasn't appealing.

I wondered, "Weren't there any other options? Couldn't I somehow create an ideal life with work I enjoyed through following the yearning for freedom that was inside me?"

ADVENTURE IN CHINA

This guide offers an alternative to working a 40-hour-a-week job as a career path and lifestyle—that is teaching English 20 hours a week, traveling through Asia, learning Mandarin Chinese, and turning these experiences into work you can be proud of and enjoy. It's not an easy path and you may feel uncomfortable at times, but if you crave adventure you will feel alive like you've never felt alive before.

This guide will help you on this path and give you some starting points and direction. It doesn't cover everything about living in China, for that several books would be needed. Instead this guide's purpose is to give you a good taste of what living in China can offer and how to go about creating this type of life for yourself.

CHAPTER 2

THE LIFE OF A FOREIGNER IN CHINA

A TYPICAL DAY IN CHINA

TUCKED IN BETWEEN HUNDRED-YEAR-OLD Guangdong architecture of southern China, there is a small Xinjiang restaurant. Xinjiang is famous for its lamb and it's for this reason that my Chinese friend Tommy and I have chosen to have supper here. It is near the end of December and both of us have two months of vacation coming up. It is standard for foreign English teachers at Chinese colleges and universities to have four months of vacation per year, which provides ample time for traveling. We are planning a road trip around Qinghai province, a part of the Tibetan plateau, over 1,000 kilometers from Guangdong province.

"We can stay with my family in Xining before we set out," says Tommy. Xining is the capital of Qinghai and Tommy's home. "We'll make that our base, and then we can head to the Kunlun Mountains and beyond."

We pay our bill, a mere 100 RMB ($15). This is enough money for both of us to eat like kings: skewers of lamb, fresh asparagus lettuce, and a couple lamb dishes.

5

I bid farewell to my friend because I'm meeting a date for a post-dinner stroll through the park. I hail a motorbike taxi for 6 RMB ($1) and have the driver take me two kilometers to the park where my date, Jing Jing, is meeting me. Jing Jing is from Zhongshan, the medium-sized city where I live and teach English. Given the sheer amount of single women in China, especially in a booming city like Zhongshan, it is no wonder I eventually met someone I could have a relationship with. Even though her English is not perfect and my Mandarin is far from perfect, we are able to communicate very well.

We stroll beneath the palm trees and other subtropical foliage on a circuit passing some small lakes within the park. Although it is December, it is still warm enough that in the evening all that is needed to stay warm is a light jacket.

"Do you want to go meet some of my friends later?" I ask Jing Jing. "They're at a club across the river."

"Why the hell not?" replies Jing Jing.

That's the kind of answer I like to hear.

We hop in a cab and take it to a club called Visa. We walk up the steps past young hipsters and check our things. The hipster crowd in China is growing year after year and these young people can be found at clubs all over China.

The music inside is perfect for drinking and dancing. The neon blue and orange lights make everyone feel like they are in a club in London or New York. Many of China's smaller towns (five million or less) have such clubs whose decor and level of hipness compete with those of some of the most well known metropolises around the world.

We make for a table where my friends are standing. Dean and Ken, two of my closest Chinese friends are there to greet us.

"Where have you guys been?" Dean asks us. "It's almost midnight!"

"We were waiting until it was busy enough. Now is the best time," I yell over the music.

Dean is the leader of a group of volunteer students assigned to help foreign teachers at the college where I teach adjust to life in China. We share a penchant for making short films and learning languages. He is from the nearby city of Shenzhen, the fourth biggest city in China, a city that 30 years ago was no more than a village.

"Who is this?" Ken asks me. He puts his hand out to shake Jing Jing's hand and introduces himself.

Ken is from one of the inner provinces of China. Although the college he goes to is not very renowned, he has been accepted into a PhD program at a different university. This is a very prestigious achievement in China that very few people ever attain.

"This is my girlfriend, Jing Jing," I tell him.

Ken does a double take as he shakes Jing Jing's hand. "Wow, she's really hot!" Ken says.

Jing Jing laughs.

We sing and dance as the servers go around pouring more green tea whiskeys for everyone. As it nears 2 a.m., the crowd starts to die down a little. We all get into cabs and head home. I have class the next day at 2:00 p.m. It's still only Monday and I love my schedule this semester.

WHY LIVE IN CHINA

I hope that the previous section was able to illustrate some of the reasons why a foreigner living in China teaching English can lead a great life. The opportunities that teaching English in China allows are many and illustrating these opportunities and how to grab them is the primary purpose of this guide.

Teaching English is the ideal way to meet and interact with the Chinese people. Some of my best friends to this day are those I met through the college where I taught.

They were students or teachers or friends of those students and teachers. I guarantee if you come to China, you will make great friends.

With less than 20 required class hours per week, there is plenty of time to explore the city you live in and hang out with friends or work on other endeavors. The four months of paid vacation gives ample time to explore this region of the world, whether it be riding a motorcycle through southeast Asia for a few bucks a day or downhill skiing in Japan. If you are interested in learning Mandarin, teaching English is a great option. Many colleges may provide free classes and a good class activity with your students is having them teach you Chinese. In addition to all of this, living in China for a year or two is a good "career" booster. The free time also allows you to work on your own entrepreneurial or artistic endeavors.

China is now the world's biggest economy and it continues to grow. Yes, there is still poverty in many places in China, but what the Chinese have accomplished in the past few decades is astounding with the creation of hundreds of millions of middle class citizens. China is truly a magnificent scene to watch unfold. I recommend everyone at least give China a look.

Now that you are curious about what life in China can offer, let's see how such a life can be attained.

CHAPTER 3

TEACHING IN A COLLEGE OR UNIVERSITY

WHY TEACH ENGLISH IN CHINA

"HOW WAS GEORGE ABLE to get into the forbidden city?" I asked my class.

"He had a picture of Jerry's girlfriend, Man Hands, who he told a girl was his dead fiancé," answered one of my favorite students in the class, So-so.

"Good. And where did he meet this girl?"

"They met at the company where Kramer pretended to work. She was the secretary," a boy in the back said.

"Good. And what was Elaine's role in this episode and how did that tie in?"

"She is friends with Bizarro Jerry and was always with him and his friends this episode, so that's why Jerry felt lonely," said another student.

The lesson that day had been looking at stories and what makes a good story. One of the elements of a good *Seinfeld* episode (which is all of them) is that the story lines of each

9

of the main characters tie together at the end of each episode, creating a strong comedic effect.

That semester the students created their own scripts, filmed their own movies, and edited them. Each of the students created a scenario where one or several of them forgot how to speak Chinese and could only rely on other languages. In the end, all of the stories tied together in that their teacher, myself, had sabotaged each of them somehow, making them unable to speak their native language.

Although no *Seinfeld* episode, the final product was fun to create, many of the classes were held someplace on campus or in the city, and the students and I both ended up doing a lot of good group work in English. As an English teacher at a college in China, you will usually have full reign to do whatever you want in class, as I was able to. Textbooks are often not even provided anyway.

Teaching English at a college or University is the ideal job for someone whose main motivation in coming to China is experiencing the place and people, learning Mandarin, traveling, starting their own business, or just having lots of free time to do what you like. One does not need to hold a degree in English or teaching and you do not need to speak Mandarin. You simply need to be able to speak English with native proficiency. In all of the universities I am familiar with, there are 10 to 20 hours of class per week and four months of paid vacation: January, February, July, and August. You will need to prepare lessons outside of class, but people usually get better at this over time and you will be able to create enough lessons in advance so that when the new semester or new year comes, you will be able to improve upon and reuse what you did the previous semester, freeing up even more time to do the things you love. Colleges and universities often include a rent-free apartment on the school premises as part of your salary and benefits package.

The main benefit to teaching English is that there is no better way to get to know China's culture and its people. Through teaching English, you will learn a lot about what it is like being Chinese in China in the modern age.

THE CLASSROOM EXPERIENCE

It was the last day of class my first week teaching English in China. My first few classes were somewhat terrifying, but now I was finding my groove. I had done the lesson I was about to do five times already and was confident in my abilities. As soon as I walked in the door, the students gave a gasp and started applauding. People muttered phrases of *ku* and *shuai*, meaning "cool" and "handsome." Applause like this for a foreign teacher in China is not uncommon, as are people calling you handsome or beautiful despite average looks.

I started the class by writing my name on the board. Before I could write out Mr. Lenczewski (len-chess-key), a rather extroverted and jovial girl in the front row shouted, "You are Mr. Handsome." The class erupted in laughter.

Mr. Handsome, it was somewhat funny and the students meant well. What the hell, I could be Mr. Handsome for this one class. I proceeded with my first lesson as I had with my other classes and had the students introduce each other in pairs, telling me their English name, where they were from, and a bit about themselves.

The girl who had dubbed me Mr. Handsome in the front row introduced herself as Fire Law, and given her fiery demeanor and hair like Buckwheat in the old *The Little Rascals* TV show, I thought it was pretty fitting. She would not be the last student in my classes with an interesting English name.

Student Backgrounds

Depending on your class, your students may come from all

over China or just the province where you teach. Most of my students were from Guangdong province in which Zhongshan, the city where I taught English, is located. However, there were a few classes where it seemed like every student was from a different Chinese province. I primarily taught freshmen, sophomores, and juniors, as seniors had fewer classes than other grades and typically did not have any foreign teachers. My students were between the ages of 18 and 22. School in China follows the same ages as in the United States. The students are ages six to 18 from kindergarten to twelfth grade, and 18 to 22 in college.

I have taught both English major and non-English major classes and the difference is typically very striking. Those who are English majors, as a whole have much better English than those who are not English majors. In a class of thirty English majors there will probably only be one or two students with whom it will be hard to communicate. In a class of non-English majors, it can be up to 25 percent.

That being said, all Chinese students are usually able to read, write, and listen much better than they can speak. This is because they have a lot of practice in these three forms of communication, but very little experience with speaking.

In the non-English major classes, you will still find some students with excellent English, and in fact these students can be some of the most enthusiastic, since they don't get chances to speak with a foreign teacher as much as English major students. I prefer to teach English majors as we can talk about a wider variety of topics, but I have also had some excellent non-English major classes filled with enthusiastic students.

English Names

As I mentioned above, many students will have great English names. I've had students with names such as Santa,

Yoyo, Kobe Bryant, Cat, Everyday, Swallow, Water, Windy, Mirko, Vemen, and Sincerely, and met one doctor named Half Passed Eight or Eight Thirty for short. Students pick English names because, among other reasons, it can be hard for a foreigner to remember all of their Chinese names since they sound very similar to the untrained ear. However, many students opt not to choose an English name.

A TYPICAL LESSON

Before I explain how you might conduct your classes and how to prepare for those classes, I will give an example of how I usually prepare for and teach class.

It's the night before class and I have not decided on the type of lesson I will use with my two classes the next day. Each class consists of about 30 students and I know I can do the same lesson with each of my two classes. Over the last few months, I've built up a great repertoire of lessons and I find that when I bring some variety and spontaneity to each 90 minute class, the results are usually better: the students enjoy the class more and speak more, and I enjoy the classes more and don't exhaust myself.

Recently I had a conversation with a friend about the days when we used to work on a farm during our college years. I realize my classes haven't heard these stories yet and decide to tell some of them. I will talk freely for the first 20 minutes, telling tales of chain sawing, bulldozing, and avoiding getting kicked by horses to generate interest in the topic. I then prepare a few questions related to farming and put them in a Word document which I save on the flash drive I always have ready for class. The questions will be used in a group discussion which will take about 30 minutes. I decide we will do a fill-in-the-blank exercise to a song from *Aladdin*. That should take about 30 minutes. I am now prepared for class.

The next morning before class, I stop in a printing shop outside the school and make enough copies of the *Aladdin* song for every student in both classes that day. Some students greet me on the walk to class with shouts of "Mr. L.", "Nick", and "Mr. Handsome".

I begin the lesson by talking about a story of getting a tractor stuck in the mud and being yelled and cursed at by my employer before he helps me get it out. After everyone is charged up, I split them into groups of four and display the questions for them to talk about on the overhead. I walk around the room listening to the students' stories.

"I grew up on a farm in Anhui province. We only made 100 *yuan* ($15) per month at that time. My parents worked in factories in Shanghai and I went to school in the village," one of my students explains to the group.

After the students had spoken for about 30 minutes, we come back together and I explain the next activity. After handing out the lyrics, I play the music from *Aladdin*. I play it through several times giving the students enough chances to hear it, and then we go through the lyrics as a group, going over the meaning of each of the more difficult words.

The bell rings, signaling the end of class.

The students were exposed to lots of new topics, vocabulary, activities, and I thought the class went well. It could be argued that they should go into more depth and I agree that it would be good. But, I only saw each class 16 times per semester and I believe that providing a good environment for students to practice English and learn about my home country's people and culture through me is the better choice.

LESSON PLANNING

You can reuse lessons, so it is in your interest to develop lesson plans that work. Some people will want to create rigid lesson plans, others may like a more flexible style (like me), but whatever route you choose, I recommend being prepared and professional when you show up for class. You do not need to have everything laid out in detail, but it's good to have a general plan. The better you get at this and the more prepared you are, the more easily you will be able to mentally prepare for a class in five minutes the night before your lessons. You can use the same lesson plans with multiple classes, so it is a good idea to spend some time creating quality lessons in the beginning.

Lesson Ideas

There are many resources online, both traditional and un-traditional to use for classes. One of the best things to do when teaching is "borrowing" other people's material and tailoring it to fit your style and the situation. Some class-rooms will have a computer, projector, and speakers (though rarely Internet connectivity in my experience), while others may only have a white board or black board. In my case, we had computers and projectors, but it was always a toss up as to whether they would be working that day.

Classes generally go well when you are talking about something you are interested in or tailoring a lesson to fit your style. Sometimes the more you prepare, the better the class will go. Sometimes the less you prepare, the better it will go. If you are trying though, it will generally go better than if you are not trying. Just don't overwork yourself. Once you get in the classroom and try some different things, you will start to learn how best to proceed. You will probably need to bomb in a few classes before you start to get the hang of it.

First, I will discuss the topics I generally use for inspiration. You should be aware of inspiration everywhere and try to use it to create lessons. Although you will probably reach a point when you have all the lessons you could ever need, I find that I get bored of lessons easily the more I teach them, which affects how well the class goes, so I am always on the lookout for potential new lessons.

Group Discussion

One of the most common activities I use is group discussion. Students feed off of the teacher's enthusiasm. Some of the best classes I've had are those where I told the students a story from my upbringing and then had them tell each other their own stories.

"I used to have a pet dog once," one of my students told me when I came and spoke with their group. The day's topic was pets. "My neighbors were hungry though and they stole him and ate him," she said with the same disbelief that crossed my own face.

Although sometimes their stories will be strange and sad, if the students are speaking English and enjoying it, then keep doing whatever it is you're doing.

When you can capture the students' attention through your own passion for something and they get into their own discussions of similar experiences, the energy is awesome.

Some of the topics I frequently used in order to facilitate discussions were stories about a farm I worked on, high school, college, and world travel. They are very interested in this last topic because few have done it yet, especially when you show them it's not as expensive as they may think (most of them are unaware of the existence of hostels and think you need to stay in an expensive hotel when you travel).

I typically prepare four or five questions for each person in the group to talk about and then float around the room, speaking with each group. You will learn a lot about Chinese culture and the students during these types of lessons. Try to think of personal topics. When all else fails, the topics of relationships and dating are the best to use as they create the most interest. Use these topics often to generate lots of chatter.

Music

Music is another great option for a lesson. Your goal can be to have students listen and sing along with whatever song you are playing. Sometimes I will bring a guitar to class and sing a song for them to sing along to. I print out lyrics for the class or display lyrics on an overhead projector. I recommend choosing music you enjoy, with lyrics that aren't too fast. If you can't understand the lyrics yourself, don't choose the song.

Sometimes I print the lyrics to a song with 10 to 20 words removed and create a fill-in-the-blank activity.

You should always have lyrics and audio files of songs ready on a flash drive so that you may use them for any class at any time with little or no planning ahead of time. Depending on how well you would like the students to learn a song, this can take up 10 to 40 minutes of class time.

Skits and Talent Shows

Another great activity, which can end up taking a full class period, or 90 minutes, is a skit or show. For the first part of class, students work in groups of two to four people, creating dialogues and skits. I usually provide some sort of prompt for each group, which I have prepared beforehand. Many websites offer such prompts.

For the second half of class, the students perform their skits or their talent if it is a talent show. Talents usually include singing, dancing, playing guitar or putting on a show.

If the class is very large (50 students or more), you may need to break up the talent show into multiple class periods. You may want to give students in the audience some sort of activity so they pay more attention, such as having everyone vote on the best performance, most dedicated performers, etc.

Students will often tell you they are not ready yet when

you ask them to perform. This is sometimes okay, but be aware that some students will use this as an excuse.

Idioms and Slang

I like to spend five to 15 minutes teaching students different phrases or slang each day. Giving example sentences is one of the best ways to teach new vocabulary or phrases. After teaching new phrases, have students create their own sentences using the new words. You may also have them create skits using different slang or situations that you have introduced to them that day.

Reading Stories

Reading lessons should be used sparingly. The point of the foreign teacher's class is to get students speaking English. However, it is also about teaching them your home country's culture. Therefore, a good children's book that the students can read along with you can be good every few classes.

One lesson I used was to have the students read Native American myths from a Power Point presentation. Then I had them answer questions about the story in small groups. I was careful not to let the story become too long, and kept it to a few slides. Even a lesson like this can take an hour or more.

Writing Exercises

Writing lessons should be used even less than reading lessons in my opinion. However, it can be very interesting for everyone to have students keep "journals" where they spend five to 10 minutes writing on a particular topic once a week. Reading these journals will give you some great insights into Chinese culture. Some of the insights you will gain about Chinese culture will be great.

TV Shows and Movies

I sometimes show English TV shows or movies in class as part of a lesson. If I do, I will write out three to five questions about what we are watching for them to answer. Many TV shows and movies you find in China will have both English and Chinese subtitles. This is ideal. If there are no subtitles, it may be very difficult for some students and still difficult for even your best students. If the subtitles are only in Chinese, this is not as good because the students may rely on them too much. If it is only English subtitles, this may also be acceptable, even though it will be a challenge, which is also good sometimes.

Some of my favorite shows and movies, which resonate well with my students, are *Seinfeld, The X-Files, The Shawshank Redemption, The Lord of the Rings*, and *Remember the Titans*. I generally show the film or show for 20 to 30 minutes and then let the class spend 10 minutes answering questions. We then spend 20 minutes going over the questions in groups and then as a class. As you can see this can easily take up an hour of class, and a nice game or something of that nature for the last 30 minutes rounds out a good lesson.

Resources

As you brainstorm lesson plans, the links below will be helpful. Be sure to look back at your own books, music, films, and TV shows for inspiration. Think of activities you did in school in classes like English, art, and foreign languages. Get as creative as you want. I've had classes where students create their own games or we learn to play American football.

As mentioned previously, be sure to have a flash drive or two to store all of the resources you find and create and bring to class everyday.

▪ **English as a Second Language** (www.rong-chang.
com)

An ESL (English as a Second Language) website containing vocabulary, dialogues, sound clips, role-plays and more.

▪ **OMG!美语** (www.youtube.com/user/OMGmeiyu)

Meiyu means "American English" and this YouTube channel is a collection of videos of a cute Caucasian American girl with the Chinese name, *Bai Jie*, speaking Mandarin and teaching English to Chinese viewers. The videos are one to two minutes long each and teach a few slang and idioms each. Typically, there is at least one new video per week.

▪ **Dave's ESL Cafe** (www.eslcafe.com/ideas/)

In addition to being a good place to start a job hunt for English teaching positions around the world, Dave's ESL Cafe has many teaching ideas submitted by other teachers. I have found some good ideas on here, which I merge with ideas of mine. You may feel some of the ideas are a little lame or may not work well for your situation. This is where you will start to get good at picking and choosing from different ideas to create your own better ideas.

CLASS LENGTH

Classes are held from September through December and March through June. Each week consists of 16 to 20 classroom hours. Classes are generally an hour-and-a-half (two 45 minute classes in a row with a 10 minute break in between). The students have up to four such periods everyday and there is a two-and-a-half-hour break for lunch and napping in the middle of the day. The first class of the day starts at 8:00 a.m. and the last class finishes at 6:00 p.m. As a foreign English teacher, you will probably not have more than two such classes each day, but if you do, you might also have one or two days off during the work week as well. A friend of mine only worked two days a week one semester, so she was able to travel a lot that term.

HOLIDAYS

You will get time off for holidays, but you will probably not learn the exact dates more than a month ahead of time. This can make it difficult to book plane or train tickets so be sure to ask around as the information is usually there, it just doesn't get officially released until the holiday is close. Students will probably know sooner than you will, so you may ask them.

Besides the two two-month breaks between semesters, there are also a half dozen shorter holidays throughout the year. I've listed them below and the amount of time you get off for each. Days off may vary.

- National Day: three days in October

- New Year's Day: one day in January

- Tomb Sweeping Day: one day in April

- May Holiday: one day in May

- Dragon Boat Day: one day in June

You may sometimes be told you have a "three day holiday" or "seven day holiday" coming up. If a holiday falls on a Tuesday, you will also get off Wednesday and Thursday, but you will need to work both days during the weekend. So these "three day holidays" are still a single day off, it's just that schedules are rearranged to let people have three days in a row off during the middle of the week.

Sometimes you may be told that even the days you have off for holiday will need to be made up at the end of the semester, but in my experience this is rarely followed through on and so should not be a huge concern.

SALARY

One downfall with the university or college English teaching route is that it does not pay as well as some of the other places you can teach or work. Oftentimes the salary is 5,000-8,000 RMB per month ($800-$1,300 in 2015). While this is plenty to live on in China and have a great time traveling around Asia, you will not be saving a lot unless you make that a primary goal. But realistically, you are only working the hourly equivalent of four months at a full time job with 40 hours a week and two weeks of vacation per year, so your hourly rate of pay is probably higher than your friends back home making $20 per hour or less. Vacations and semester breaks are also paid.

Most schools will also provide housing so there is no need to rent an apartment. Most on-campus housing I have encountered, either my own or friends', has been good. More on apartments later.

In addition to the salary and apartment, most schools will reimburse your airfare. When looking at positions (which we'll discuss later), make sure the school you are applying to reimburses for airfare as round-trip airfare is typically around 10,000 RMB ($1,500) from North America.

CHINESE EDUCATION SYSTEM

I always have to laugh to myself when the United States media uses Chinese students to try to motivate our own students. Though there are many students in China who are quite exemplary in their studies and on the whole Chinese households place more of an emphasis on education than in the United States, the Chinese education system is not as advanced as the United States' in terms of teaching its students the abilities to create and think critically. The Chinese education system may instill other valuable skills that the United States does not do as well at (such as memorization), but overall I think China has more to learn from the United States about education than the reverse.

In comparison to classes in the United States where there is a lot of student participation, classes throughout the education system in China seem to primarily consist of the Chinese teacher speaking to the students, the students memorizing facts, and then taking exams. There is little participation on the part of the students, creativity is not encouraged, critical thinking is not encouraged, and therefore students may be hesitant to participate in your class. It is a foreign concept to them.

As to the reasons for this, I cannot say, but certainly some of them include the teacher-student ratio, China's large population, and the immediate need for an educated work force. A weird part of Chinese education in colleges is that students cannot fail a class. If you fail a student, you will be required to give them a make up test until they pass. For this reason, you may want to consider giving the lowest passing grade to the students who are failing.

I'm still not exactly sure why this is, but I believe it has to do with the fact that parents and families are paying for a student and therefore the student should be able to graduate. I could be wrong.

Chinese Teacher Class vs. Foreign Teacher Class
It is important to know that as a foreign English teacher, your class will be very different from almost every other class the students have had in their lives. Some students will have had foreign teachers in the past in high school or middle school but for many students your class will be their first taught by a native English speaker.

The Chinese teacher's classes focus mainly on rote memorization. Students are not asked for their input, don't speak much in class to the teacher or each other, and the Chinese teacher does almost all of the talking.

In your class, students will be expected to participate and make mistakes. They will not be familiar with this and many will be apprehensive about doing so. Be patient with them and find creative ways to get them to speak. It's not that they don't want to speak, but it's uncomfortable for many of them. The concept of "face" may be a big part of this.

Face

The concept of face in China is extremely important. Face is about preserving good standing in the eyes of one's group (classmates, family, coworkers, etc.). Making a mistake while trying to pronounce an English word correctly in front of your classmates can easily bring laughs, ridicule, and a loss of face. It is important to let students know that your class is different and that making mistakes is part of learning to speak a foreign language. They are learning a different culture, one where face is not as important. However, you are in their culture and will need to be very accommodating.

At first I was confused by the concept of face, as many people are when they come to China. In the end, it boils down to being considerate of the other person and not being loud, obnoxious, or rude. Groups in China are very important and a group of students is like a close-knit group that is continually helping itself and not letting itself look bad. Sometimes this may feel superficial or inefficient to you, but try to just go with it.

Discipline

Some of your classes will be amazing and some will be classes from hell. It can be easy to be too hard on yourself when a student criticizes your method and it is equally easy to be too easy on yourself when students are walking all over you. In my experience, the cultural gap can distort what is real and what is not, so a certain amount of accounting for biases is necessary.

Students can be better in how they treat their foreign teacher compared to their Chinese teachers, as well as worse. Some students will see your class as a joke (though these students probably see all their classes as a joke), and others will treasure you and your class.

Times will come when you need to discipline your classes. I did not do this as much in the beginning of my teaching career and there were definitely a few classes that got out of hand because of this.

Students should not be talking when you are talking. This is disrespectful. A Chinese teacher would never tolerate this and most students wouldn't even dare to do it in their Chinese teachers' classes.

If a student is disruptive, I recommend taking that student aside after class and speaking with them about their behavior. Try not to let other students see this, as you don't want to make them lose face in front of others. If the student continues to act up, speak with someone in the department who can help. I once had a student who yelled loudly and always spoke blatantly in Mandarin to no one in particular when I was explaining an activity. I ended up yelling at him one day in front of everyone (which I somewhat regret), but he never spoke again or disturbed the class for the remainder of the year. He also didn't participate and therefore did poorly, but that was better than having him disrupting the class.

TEACHING TIPS
Before ending this section, I want to share with you some useful philosophies for teaching classes picked up over six years spent teaching English in China. They can be very useful and may prove critical to your success. They were definitely critical to my success as a teacher.

TIP 1: Save your energy

You shouldn't be talking for the entire class, this will wear you out. The more that the students are talking (in English) the better. In the beginning you will need to be passionate to get them excited to do an activity. Work to find a balance between using your energy to motivate the students, and taking a backseat and watching them go.

TIP 2: Always pay attention to the students' level of interest

Don't let a topic or activity go on for so long that it gets to the point where most students are bored. It's a good idea to stop an activity near the peak of excitement or right after the peak (this is generally when the most laughing and smiling is seen). Of course you also want to the students to enjoy the activities, especially when they are into it! It may seem cruel to stop sometimes, but follow your intuition and stop them just when things seem to be dying down a bit. This way, students will be more excited when you do the same activity or a similar activity again in a future class.

TIP 3: Take student suggestions with a grain of salt

It's common for foreign teachers to ask their students what they would like to learn and it may seem like a good idea, but generally the students will give you the same answers every time: your own culture, movies, music, sports. These are usually too vague of ideas to work with. Therefore, I recommend doing the things you find interesting. The students will probably find those topics the most interesting.

There will also always be some students that don't like what you've decided to do, but in general, these students won't like anything, no matter what the lesson is, so try not to worry about them too much. Always try to include them, but realize that it's not you, it's them.

TIP 4: Float around the class
You should spend a good amount of time floating around the class trying to speak with each student. If they are answering questions together or doing an activity, sit down with them and take the place of one of the students in the group and ask different questions or answer their questions.

TIP 5: Balance
Much of teaching is about balance between doing too much and too little. Pay attention to the reactions of students. Don't sell yourself short and don't cater to the disruptive or "problem" students. Focus on hearing lots of English spoken, and on laughs, and you'll be great.

Teaching is considered an art, and it is one of the highest and most difficult of art forms in my opinion.

TIP 6: Offer encouragement
Many students will be discouraged or not able to speak English very confidently. Tell them that you understand and tell them how difficult it is for you when learning a foreign language. Make them feel you understand them. Be patient with them and try to give them more opportunities to speak. The Chinese culture is short on encouragement in general and a little bit can go a long way. Students have told me that their parents have never told them that they love them (not because they don't, but because it's not verbalized). However, they tell me they really appreciate it when I encourage them.

Most importantly, in this author's opinion you'll find that while your students will be learning a lot from you, you will end up learning much more from them.

CHAPTER 4

TEACHING IN OTHER INSTITUTIONS

TEACHING IN K-12 SCHOOLS

IN THE PREVIOUS SECTION, I mainly drew on my three years of experience as a college English teacher. However, teaching college English is not the only option you have when coming to China to teach English.

In the following section, I will outline other avenues of employment including working at K-12 schools (kindergarten through twelfth grade) and English training centers, also known as cram schools. A lot of the information in the previous section about teaching will also apply when teaching at these other institutions, therefore this section will be brief in comparison.

Fashion Show

"This is Coco, she's wearing a blue dress and white shirt," one of my second grade students says about her class partner as Coco struts up and down the main aisle of the classroom like a model. "She is very beautiful."

For a class activity we were having a fashion show, which entailed students in groups of two introducing what each other was wearing as one of them walks up and down the aisles like a model. I would typically put on some music by Madonna or Cascada, or "Gangsta's Paradise" and I found that almost any music works well.

I was not able to find as many varied activities as I was for my college students, but during the six months I taught primary school students, I did develop my own effective method of teaching.

Types of Lessons

In the example above, we made an activity out of the topic of clothing. Many of the topics you will cover in a primary school will be relatively simple: food, colors, sports, classroom objects, etc. I find it easiest to expand from a particular topic where vocabulary has already been covered and make it into a simple activity or activities.

As you get into middle school and high school classes the vocabulary will develop further and other topics such as careers and the sciences will be added.

The Chinese English Teacher

As with college, the students will have a Chinese English teacher who is their primary English teacher. Unlike college though, you will rely heavily on them for discipline and class content. The Chinese teacher usually stays in the classroom, helps with the activities, and provides order in the class. I've had some classes where the teacher is good and keeps students on task with a series of mind tricks (point systems, clapping, standing up and sitting down), and I have also had classes where the teacher doesn't do much and the students need to be quieted down every three minutes for the entire hour.

In middle schools and high schools, the Chinese English

teacher will play a smaller role and you will need to fend for yourself most of the time. Fortunately, the students are also more aware and respectful.

Lesson Planning

When preparing for class, you may be able to use a text-book, which someone at the school will have given to you ahead of time. The textbook will contain some vocabulary and dialogues, which you will be able to incorporate into your lesson.

For the first part of the lesson, you may want to review vocabulary with the students, letting them hear your pro-nunciation, and having them repeat it. The important part will be going over sentence structures and substituting vo-cabulary into sentences covered in the dialogue. You can even make this into an activity if time allows. For more advanced classes (fifth and sixth grades), I had a "My Fa-vorite" activity where students were able to tell me their favorites in a given category.

"My favorite video game is Final Fantasy VII," I would start. They would then tell me their favorite video games one by one. King of Fighters and CS (Counter Strike) were usually the all around favorites in 2011. I'm curious to know what they are as of 2015.

As with college students, you will want to prepare les-sons ahead of time so that you are composed in class and able to help students individually.

I find that with middle school and high school students, the topics I used for college students were very good be-cause the students were younger and so had not heard the topics before. For example, the topic of dating was extra popular in high school and middle school because teachers never talk about it.

In addition to the lessons I have already mentioned and those I have covered in the college section, the below games may be particularly helpful when working with younger students.

Hangman is a good game to play with students of any age, even college students (for them you may want to try phrases instead of just words). Younger students will like Hangman and it is great for filling in five to 15 minutes of class at the end of the day. Make sure students raise their hand before giving a letter.

Charades is a great game to play with young students because they like to move around in class. In one class, I once had a realistic Michael Jackson impression from an eight year old when the word was "dance". If you don't know how charades works, it is a game where you show a student a word or phrase and then they need to mime it for the class without making any noise. The students then guess the word.

Student Backgrounds

Unlike in college, your students will generally be from the city you live in. Most schools are not free in China and parents are paying for their children to go to school.

Students in primary school are between ages six and 12. Middle school goes from grade seven through nine and students are 13 through 15 years old. Students in high school are ages 16 through 18.

As the students get older, they will generally have better English skills and a wider vocabulary. Students have a lot of pressure in middle school and high school to prepare for the *gaokao*. The *gaokao* is like the SAT or ACT in the United States, but much more intense. Everything the student has learned up until this point will be tested and the results of the test will determine which schools they are able to go to. It can also only be taken once per year.

Therefore, when you are teaching high school students,

you may not get all the attention you would like in class since your class will not help them with their exams.

Class Length

Classes are generally about an hour in length. If you are not teaching, you probably don't need to be present at the school. You will probably only have about twenty hours of classroom teaching per week. Classes are held from about 8:00 a.m.–12:00 p.m., 2:30 p.m.–5:00 p.m., and then once more in the evening from 7:30 p.m.–9:00 p.m. This last session can be more like a study hour sometimes, but the students are typically still required to go.

Holidays

Students in primary, middle, and high school have a similar schedule to those in college. They get the same holidays as the rest of the country, but their semester breaks are shorter than those of the college students.

They will not usually get four full months off per year and generally only have six weeks off in the winter and six weeks off in the summer.

Salary

Your salary as a primary, middle, or high school teacher will be comparable to what you earn as a college teacher. It will be somewhere in the range of 5,000 to 8,000 RMB per month unless you are in a big city like Shanghai in which case it could be more.

Teaching Tips

All of the same tips I gave in the college teaching section still apply, however, students will generally have shorter attention spans than in college, especially if the content is more intellectual. It is important to meet the students on their level.

TEACHING AT A TRAINING CENTER

Besides K-12 schools and colleges, there is also a third type of school where foreign English teachers are in high demand: training centers.

Training centers are schools where anyone can go to take extra English classes from both Chinese and foreign teachers. With more and more Chinese moving into the middle class and with the high emphasis on education in China it is no surprise that many kids spend hours every Saturday and Sunday at these types of schools when they aren't at their normal school.

In addition to parents putting their kids in training centers for extra English classes, many working adults are learning English at such schools in order to better their life, sometimes for work and sometimes for pure enjoyment.

These schools all want to hire foreign teachers because the demand for them is high. It is seen as a good thing in China to have your son or daughter being taught by a foreigner, and many adult students respect their foreign teacher a lot. Adult student classes are some of my favorite classes to teach because all of these students really want to be there and they have more life experiences they can share with you.

In this section, I will explain everything you need to know about training centers.

Student Backgrounds

The main determinant of what a class will be like is the age of the students. Many of the lessons from previous sections can also be used in training centers. Oftentimes training centers will provide a textbook of decent quality, which can be used for part of the lesson. Sometimes you may even receive some direction from the staff on what to teach, though usually you will still have a lot of power to do what you like in class.

Primary School Students
Lessons can be similar to those used in primary school. Your group will be somewhere between five and 20 students, depending on how busy the day is. It will be rare that every student who has signed up for your class will be at every class, so be prepared for a wide range of attendees on any given day.

When I teach in training centers I typically teach a lesson from the textbook that involves speaking and have students answer the prompts in the textbook. For the other half of class we do an activity related to the text and one to my own culture. If there is time at the end, we play a game.

Middle School and High School Students
There will be more middle school students in your classes than high school students because parents of high school students will have them studying for their *gaokao* so they can get into a good college instead of learning oral English.

Middle school students can be taught in the same way as they are taught in middle school. There will be a smaller group and you will have more chances to work with each student individually. Try to gauge your lessons to fit their demographic. It may take a few lessons with each class in order to determine this.

Adult Students
I have never taught college students at a training center, and though they may attend classes, it's doubtful that you will teach any. However, you will probably teach students that have jobs and are the same age or much older than you. Most of these students are in their twenties, thirties,

and early forties. Besides college students, adult students are my favorite age range to teach.

Their backgrounds will be quite varied. I've taught factory workers, doctors, housewives, and entrepreneurs all in the same class.

For these classes, I typically do the same lessons I do with college students, but at the same time I will think about how English will help them in their work and life. They are usually paying their own money to be in class so the level of participation will often be higher than in non-adult classes. You may even make some good friends through these classes.

Class Length

Class length in training centers is similar to those of colleges and universities: two 45 minute lengths of class with a 10 minute break in between. The main thing that is different between these classes and those taught in colleges or K-12 schools is the time of day the classes are held and the days of the week.

Training centers have classes every day of the week, but the busiest days are Saturday and Sunday when kids are off from school. Classes are held all day Saturday and Sunday with five or six periods each day. Classes during the week are held in the evening and there are either one or two periods each night.

Some schools will hire you full time, while other schools will hire you part time. I have only ever worked part time so I would typically teach only one or two times at a center each week.

In addition to teaching at different times throughout the week, the times of year that are the busiest are during winter break and summer break, when students are off from school. For these six weeks, training centers are in operation all day every day and have several periods each day.

Holidays

Usually, for the same holidays that K-12 schools and colleges have, training centers too will not be in operation. In fact many types of businesses all over China will also not be open on these days. The exception to this is summer and winter breaks as I mentioned above. This will be the busiest time for training centers.

Salary

Training center salaries will vary depending on the establishment and whether you work full time or part time. If you work full time, 15,000-20,000 RMB salaries in bigger cities is normal. For this though you will be working full time year round and may need to be on site all 40 hours every week. You will still probably only be teaching about twenty hours a week, but may have other responsibilities as well. In the bigger cities you can likely find even higher pay.

If you are teaching part time, then you will probably be paid between 100 and 200 RMB per hour.

CONCERNING TEACHING

One final word about teaching. Your experience teaching will be very different depending on the age of the students you teach, the subject you teach, and where you teach. A teacher at a college in the United States will have a different experience teaching biology in her own country than she will as a primary school English teacher working in a small city in Sichuan province. The two jobs require very different skill sets.

If you enjoy working with kids, teaching in a primary school is a good route for you. If you enjoy having intellectual conversations, then teaching in a college or teaching adults in a training center is a better fit.

Whatever route you decide to pursue, you are guaranteed

to learn a lot from your students and make some great friendships.

CHAPTER 5

WHERE TO LIVE

THE IMPORTANCE OF LOCATION

NOW THAT YOU KNOW more about what teaching English in China is like and you're interested in learning what else living in the middle kingdom has to offer, you need to find a job. One of the most important factors that go into choosing a job is location. It is also very important for living and working in general.

In this section, I offer an overview of the main pros and cons of living in bigger-sized cities, medium-sized cities, small cities, and how cities are laid out. Since cities like Macau and Hong Kong are not really the same as the rest of China's cities, I will leave them for the end.

Besides the school you will work at, things to consider when choosing a city are the location, population, climate, and level of economic development.

CITY TIERS

Every city in China belongs to a certain tier level. Beijing, Shanghai, Guangzhou, and Shenzhen are all first tier cities in China. They're also the only cities besides Hong

Kong that might be considered international cities. They each have over 10 million people and are more developed compared with the rest of China's cities. There are more job opportunities in bigger cities and therefore also more expatriates (expats). There are more services catering to foreigners: restaurants, shops selling foreign products, etc. Generally these cities will be cleaner and nicer than smaller cities.

All other provincial capitals in China are considered second tier cities. Chengdu, Hangzhou, Chongqing, and Nanjing are examples of such cities. These cities also have many of the same aspects of life as the first tier cities and are great bets for foreigners wanting to live and work in China. There are many job opportunities here too and these are also the fastest growing cities in China.

I have spent all of my time in China living in third tier cities (Zhongshan, Jiaxing, Jiangmen). These cities are medium-sized (one to five million people) and are more developed than towns and villages. They usually don't have as many foreigners or services catering to foreigners, and there are less jobs than in bigger cities, however you should not overlook them. There are hundreds of these types of cities and I find that each is unique and generally has more character than the bigger cities. There is something appealing about living in a city the size of Chicago that few people have heard of. The third tier cities like Zhongshan can also be very clean, especially if they are in Guangdong, one of the cleanest provinces in China.

Within each city are smaller districts, which are themselves smaller cities within the municipality. In Zhongshan, the central city is called Shiqi, which is where I lived and worked. The surrounding cities of Xiaolan, Sanxiang, and Zhongshangang are all districts within the larger whole, each containing their own downtowns, shopping malls, and colleges. These cities are smaller than the central city, but also hold opportunities. Generally, there will be more for-eigners and opportunities in the central city. Within each district are dozens of villages depending on how large the area is. It's important to think about where you will live within the city as well. Where I taught in Zhongshan was an ideal set-up because where I lived and worked was in the center of the central district. I could walk to restaurants, malls, and bars within 10 or 15 minutes. I could also take a cab for 10 or 15 RMB to anywhere in the central city within 15 minutes.

In comparison, my friend once taught at a school on the outskirts of Nanchang, the biggest city in Jiangxi province. There were some restaurants, bars, and arcades around the college for students, but otherwise it was a 45-minute bus ride into the city or a 75 RMB 30 minute cab ride into the city for restaurants, malls, and bars. I advise choosing a school with a good location.

ECONOMIC DEVELOPMENT
When I first thought about moving to China, I had dreams of living on a picturesque farm and drinking tea with my neighbors every morning and evening watching the days roll by. The reality of such a life is very different and you would likely be toiling in the mud most of the day and suf-fering from severe culture shock the entire time. I'm not saying this is a certainty, or that you wouldn't enjoy such a lifestyle, but I know that a person's visions and reality can be very different things.

One of the most important things you will probably need in order to be happy in China is a built-in network of amenities (western toilets, McDonald's, a foreign foods section at the supermarket, etc.) and other foreigners. I am all for cultural immersion and no matter where you end up you will have plenty of opportunities for this. Because many of these cultural immersion experiences can become exhausting, you probably will be happier in cities that are more habitable to foreigners. You don't want to end up canceling your stay in China and going home early. You can think of China as being broken into two major areas in terms of prosperity: Eastern Coast and Interior. The provinces of Guangdong, Zhejiang, Jiangsu, and Fujian are the wealthiest. The first, second, and third tier level cities in these provinces will all be fairly developed. As you move towards the interior the bigger and smaller cities will be less and less developed.

If you are looking for adventure in one of China's smaller cities or villages, the interior is a good bet. There are lots of smaller third tier cities here that have most western amenities but are explored by few foreigners.

Almost all of China's provinces are mountainous and these areas while usually the poorest are the most beautiful. Kunming, in Yunnan, or Chengdu, in Sichuan, are good choices for someone who wants to live in a city but be close to the countryside and getaways like the Silk Road and Mount Everest.

When trying to decide where to live, I recommend reading blogs and websites about different cities. Below are some blogs and websites for reading about different cities and speaking with people who have lived in these cities or similar cities in China.

■ **EChinaCities** (www.echinacities.com)
A website for expats containing city guides, job postings, news, and more.

■ **ChengDu Living** (www.chengduliving.com)
This is a website for expats living in Chengdu, the capital of Sichuan province. There are guides, pictures, and an active forum.

- **The Beijinger** (www.thebeijinger.com)
  A website dedicated to life in Beijing.

- **Shanghai Expat** (www.shanghaiexpat.com)
  A website dedicated to life in Shanghai.

- **Far West China** (www.farwestchina.com)
  A website dedicated to Xinjiang province. Xinjiang's capital, Urumqi is the furthest large city on earth from an ocean. Xinjiang is also home to some amazing scenery.

- **The Land of Snows** (www.thelandofsnows.com)
  A website dedicated to information about Tibet. If you are thinking of living in Tibet or planning a trip there, this is an excellent resource with great photos and guides.

- **China Life Files** (www.chinalifefiles.com)
  This is my own blog, which has information on Zhongshan, Guangdong and Jiaxing, Zhejiang.

HONG KONG AND MACAU

Hong Kong and Macau are technically a part of China, but the cultures and economies are very different from mainland China's. While mainland China will feel like another world compared with where you are from, Hong Kong and Macau will have a way of life that doesn't feel too different from somewhere like London or Los Angeles. These cities both have a relatively western feel to them. This isn't to say Hong Kong lacks its Asian roots. In some ways the Chinese tradition is preserved much better in Hong Kong than it is in mainland China. Think of Hong Kong as a cross between mountainous tropical islands and New York City with Chinese culture.

The cost of living in Hong Kong is much higher than in mainland China. A very small one-bedroom apartment in an average area of Hong Kong will cost at least $1,000

USD per month and probably a lot more. Salaries however, will not be that much higher than in a city like Shanghai or Beijing.

Personally I find Macau a little boring. It can be fun if you like gambling, but otherwise it is very small.

■ **Geo Expat** (www.geoexpat.com)
A website dedicated to expat life in Hong Kong.

■ **Macau Expat** (http://macauexpatchick.com)
I have never used this guide because I have little interest in Macau, but you may want to do some research with it. I know of one person in China who makes a living off of gambling and if this sounds like something you'd be interested in, maybe Macau would be a good fit for you.

CLIMATE

Another consideration you may want to add is the climate of the area you will be moving to. Personally, I prefer a warmer climate where it doesn't snow or get too cold. I like to be able to walk around every day of the year without a coat if possible and not be stuck inside for several months out of the year. Being a huge country, both longer from north to south and east to west than the United States, China has a very diverse climate.

Southern China

Guangzhou and Hong Kong in southern China are at roughly the same latitude as Mexico City and winters are relatively mild. November through January is the ideal time to be in southern cities like Zhongshan or Shenzhen since temperatures are between 10 and 20 degrees Celsius.

Although the winters are not very cold, they are wet, and apartments in southern China are not heated very well. You will feel the cold from January to March.

The summers are hot and wet, and as it is the rainy

season between April and August, it's likely to rain a lot. The mornings are usually clear, and then around noon it will get cloudy and rain for an hour before clearing up again. Most days I would need to take a shower three to four times per day (one after every outing). It's usually about 30 degrees Celsius and very humid.

Eastern China

Shanghai is at around the same latitude as Houston, Texas, United States and it is cold in the winter. It gets snow though not a lot. Like in southern China, most of the buildings aren't heated. Space heaters are still generally used.

The summers are extremely hot though not as humid as in southern China.

Northern China

Beijing is at the same latitude as Chicago or New York and has the same weather, being hot in summer and cold in winter. As with most parts of the world these days, seasons like spring and autumn in Beijing have been reduced to four to six weeks.

Western China

During the Spring Festival winter holiday some years ago my friend and I trekked around the mountains and rubber tree plantations of Yunnan, a province abutting Tibet and Myanmar in southwestern China. Though it was cold, it only dipped below freezing during the night and the days were sunny.

We first spent time trekking through the mountains in the northern Yunnan, not far from the city of Dali, home to old women with black teeth selling marijuana (definitely worth a stop if you are needing more stories to tell your kids or future grandchildren).

After our time spent in Northern Yunnan, we flew to

the southern city of Jinghong, which is the capital of Xishuangbanna, which is at the southern tip of Yunnan and at the same latitude as Hong Kong and bordering Laos. Xishuangbanna is sometimes referred to as "China's Thailand" and it does feel and look like Thailand in many places. The weather at this time of year is amazing and around fifteen degrees Celsius.

CHOOSING A RANDOM CITY

Despite all of your efforts to find the ideal city, oftentimes going to a random city you know nothing about will end up being a great fit. This is what happened to me when I was placed in Zhongshan. In my experience, choosing a random city can provide great results—Zhongshan is easily my favorite city in the world.

CHAPTER 6

FINDING A JOB

WHERE TO LOOK

BELOW ARE SOME RESOURCES and methods for finding English teaching positions in China. Other language positions may also be listed. Positions should usually display the number of teaching hours, salary, if airfare is included, if an apartment is included, and some details about the school. Most schools will also have a website in English and you will want to look at this too.

Your Network
This is the best place to start. Whether you are currently a university student, high school student, or employee, your most valuable source for finding an English position is speaking with someone who is currently teaching English in China or has taught there previously. Even if you don't know anyone who has taught in China, someone you know will know someone who has. I suggest finding this person and speaking to them about their experience because in addition to learning about their experience, you will potentially be able to follow the same route to getting a job that they did.

University Connections

If you are currently a university student or are an alumnus, your college may have connections with teach-in-Asia programs. I first came to China through a program, which recruited people of all ages, and was usually particularly successful each year with finding future teachers through my school. My university also had other programs teaching English in China and Japan as well. So email or talk to someone where you went to college. The Asian Studies or foreign exchanges departments are good places to start.

■ **Confucius Institutes** (www.confucius.umn.edu)

Confucius Institutes are usually located near universities and are institutes for learning Chinese language and culture set up by the Chinese government. The link above is for the institute located at the University of Minnesota. The people who work at Confucius Institutes are usually educators or those who have taught or worked in China previously. Someone there will probably be able to point you in the right direction. To find the Confucius Institute in your area do an online search.

Job and Volunteer Fairs

Job and volunteer fairs will also have teacher placement programs, which place students in schools in China. The program I did was actually considered a volunteer program and I first found out about it through a volunteer fair at my university. I later attended a job fair and interviewed for a position that sent teachers to teach English in Japan. Job and volunteer fairs are both good places to meet people with placement programs who could help you get to China and work for a good school.

■ **Dave's ESL Café** (www.eslcafe.com)

This is probably the largest online community for finding English teaching jobs all over the world. There is an entire section dedicated to China since China has more English teaching positions than any other country. You will be able to look at job postings and get in touch with the recruiters at the school or agency that posted the position.

It should be noted that some of these schools and agencies can be shady and stories of foreigners landing in China for very little pay, in a backwater town that they did not want to be in are not uncommon. This is why finding someone who has done the program you are considering or taught at the school you are looking at is important.

■ **Angelina's ESL Café** (www.anesl.com)

This website is like Dave's ESL Café, but strictly for foreigners looking to teach at schools in China. I have friends who have had good success with this website and the university I taught at, Zhongshan College, also posts position openings here.

TEACHING REQUIREMENTS

Position requirements differ from school to school and therefore from agency to agency. The positions you find through agencies are a good option because they usually screen the schools that they send teachers to. Most reputable schools will require a bachelor's degree. If you have a master's degree that is excellent because you typically will be paid more. It does not matter what your area of study was and sometimes schools will even cater to your area of study and allow you teach a class in that area.

Colleges in Guangdong province require two years of teaching experience or background related to teaching. Tutoring positions that you may have held in college or substitute teaching you may have done at some point can count. China has been known to bend rules in order to accommodate everyone—and foreign English teachers are in high demand. Just be aware that restrictions on work visas have gotten stricter when it comes to hiring foreigners. If you are persistent in your desire to come to China, you will find a way. Many schools do not have a restriction on having previous teaching experience, but it depends on the school. If you are applying to a K-12 school or training center, previous jobs like nannying will also help when applying. Even if you have no teaching or nannying experience whatsoever, you can still come to China and try teaching in a training center or other school where the restrictions may not be as tight. In general, restrictions are more relaxed as one moves towards the interior of China, and into less developed cities. It is the wealthier provinces like Guangdong, Zhejiang, and Jiangsu that have tighter restrictions.

China has also been known to change its laws quickly and without warning. In 2006, before I went to China, there was a yearlong restriction on foreigners coming to China to teach English. Foreigners were required to have two years of teaching experience. When I applied to go to China in 2007, the government had removed the law, allegedly because they could not fill the demand otherwise. Unfortunately a similar law is now back in place in some provinces, like Guangdong.

Many schools like to have native English speakers (native Australians, Canadians, New Zealanders, Brits, Americans, etc.), but most will also accept non-native speakers to also teach English. I've known foreigners from Germany, Denmark, Sweden, and France that taught English in China.

If your native language is something other than English, it's also possible to teach your own native language. Languages that are also taught by foreign teachers in China include Japanese, Korean, German, French, and Spanish. Zhongshan College had two native Japanese teachers in addition to the six English-speaking teachers.

GETTING THE JOB

After you have applied to a school or program, you will need to have an interview. This will likely be over the phone or Skype if the school has no one in your country to interview you in person. If it is a placement program or agency you are interviewing with, the interview may be in person. I had my interview at my university the spring before I left for China, which was in late August.

I will talk about interviewing again in a later section about finding non-teaching jobs, but right now I also want to touch on this subject. Eighty percent of a successful interview is about preparing for the interview beforehand and being the right fit for the position.

In order to do a good job preparing, you will need to do a bit of research about the position. Looking at the job description is not enough. Some things you should do are: read about the school or company on their website, find out what their mission statement is, brainstorm ways you can contribute uniquely to the school and reasons why you are an ideal candidate, have some answers prepared for common questions (what are your strengths, what are your weaknesses, why do you want this position), and brainstorm questions to ask about the position. If you haven't had an interview in a while, or ever in the case of many college students, I recommend doing a mock interview with someone, or at the very least, write down answers to potential questions ahead of time and mentally rehearse them a few times.

Some programs or schools may do multiple interviews (one phone, one in-person), and there may be a background check, which can take a few weeks or more. Some schools and programs will want you to write in your application form answers to all of the questions I've mentioned above, so take your time with this because the more you write and think about what you are going to be doing, the better you will do in the interview. You may also find out along the way that a particular program or school is not the right fit for you.

After your interview, if you are accepted to the program, there will still be some work to do before you leave.

CHAPTER 7

PREPARING FOR CHINA

APPLY FOR A VISA

IN ORDER TO WORK legally in China, you will need to get a work visa, also known as a Z Visa. Upon arrival in China, the Z Visa is easily converted into a residence permit within your first month of living in China. However, to do this you will need to complete a lot of paper work that is best left for your employer to help you with.

One of the main things you will need when applying for your visa is previous work experience in the area of work you are planning to do in China. It is best to work with your school figuring out exactly what is needed, and if it is a good school they will coordinate everything for you. When completing this part of the application, be sure to think about all the work experiences you have had and find clever ways to rephrase your experiences (without lying) so that you come across as having had the necessary experience for whichever position you are applying for. As I have said before, try to use tutoring experiences, nannying experiences, and substitute teaching experiences if you do not have any solid teaching experience in a K-12 school or institution of higher learning.

Once you have all of the correct documentation, you will probably need to send some of it to your employer in China so that they can apply for some documents you will need when applying for a visa in your home country. They will then send you these documents, which should be submitted with your visa application in your home country. If you do not live near a consulate you may need to use a courier service. The service I typically use in the United States is My China Visa (www.mychinavisa.com).

Getting a Check-Up
One thing you may need to do before applying for a visa is have a check-up at a clinic. This is because in order to apply for a work visa, you will need some other documents from your employer, and to get these you will need to send lab test results and information from your check-up to prove that you are healthy.

BUYING PLANE TICKETS
Before applying for a visa, you may need to have your plane tickets bought already. As I've already mentioned, many schools and programs reimburse your plane ticket expenses, but you will still need to spend some money first to buy the tickets initially.

There are numerous websites out there for buying tickets, but to name a few you can try Kayak (www.kayak.com), Zuji (www.zuji.com), and Cheap Tickets (www.cheaptickets.com). You may also want to use a travel agent if you want to save time. If you are a student near the time when buying tickets, you may be able to get cheaper tickets through a website like Student Universe (www.studentuniverse.com).

PACKING

One of the main questions I get from people preparing to move to China is, "What should I bring?" You will probably be able to buy all your necessities in China and for things like clothes, I don't think you need to bring too much since you can buy a lot once there. If you are a tall person, you may want to pack some of your own clothes. I usually had to bring my own pants because I'm six feet tall and pants generally aren't long enough for me in China. Pack the equivalent for a two-week trip and then buy the rest upon arrival is my advice.

The main things you will need to bring are the things you need from your home country that you can't find in China. Below is a list of things you may not be able to find in China or that are too expensive to buy in China.

- Laptop computer
- English books
- Teaching materials (music, books, etc.)
- Mandarin textbook and phrase book
- Alarm clock
- Shoes
- Deodorant (Chinese deodorant is ineffective and Western style deodorant cannot be found in China)

Everything else, you can find in China without too much trouble. Just remember that you will probably accumulate many things while in China (clothes, souvenirs, gifts from students, etc.). When you move back to your home country, it may be difficult to take everything and shipping is expensive. Not bringing too much in the beginning will help make more room for items on the return journey. Two suitcases and a large backpack should be the limit in my opinion.

MONEY

You will probably need some money in China between when you are first paid and when you arrive in the mainland. I recommend exchanging money before you leave your home country.

The Chinese currency goes by different names, but is typically called *yuan* (said like the letters "U" and "N" pushed into one syllable). It is also called *renminbi* or RMB, meaning "the people's currency." I recommend taking out a thousand RMB for each week you are in China before you will be paid. It is cheaper than going to an ATM and withdrawing from your account once you are already there and more convenient. The exchange rate as of October 2015 is around 6.35 RMB to one US dollar.

My first school paid me at the start of each month and I only needed to wait a week or so before being paid for the first time. You shouldn't need to wait more than a month and I would guess that you'd be paid one of your first weeks in China.

Airfare reimbursement is given at different times depending on the school. Sometimes you will get it all back in a lump sum with your first paycheck. Other times you will get half with your first paycheck and half once you've been at the school for half a year.

BOOKS

One of the best ways to prepare for an adventure is to start learning about the world you plan to explore. A good and inexpensive way to do this is through books and films. Below is a list of some of the best books I have read about China, both fiction and non-fiction.

■ **China Underground by Zachary Mexico**
China Underground is a collection of stories written by Zachary Mexico based on his interviews with

various characters of the "New China." In it, he interviews a screenwriter, a prostitute, a gang leader, and a photographer among many others. It is very easy to read and my favorite part is how he writes about some characters that in the western world might be considered larger than life, but in China, are the norm. He is able to describe two disheveled villagers and their prostitutes in a hotel lobby, and then nonchalantly talk about being hungry and going to get something to eat, and portray it in a way that makes you feel like this is another typical day (which it is). Unlike many non-fiction accounts of people's experiences living in China, it is unpretentious and humorous. It's a breath of fresh air when it comes to describing the lives, dreams, and realities of people in China today.

■ Leave Me Alone by Murong

Leave Me Alone, also known as *Chengdu, Jinye Qing Jiang Wo Yiwang* (Chengdu, Please Forget About Me Tonight), is written by the Chinese author, Murong Xuecun. It is a humorous account of a twenty-something Chinese man and a few of his friends and their troubles: gambling debts, work, marriage, sex addiction, lust, and drugs. The story was first distributed online and propelled Murong into fame. He is known for being a critic of Chinese censorship.

■ The Train to Lo Wu by Jess Row

The Train to Lo Wu is a collection of short stories by Jess Row that take place in and around Hong Kong. This is one of my favorite books of all time and I have read each story numerous times. The world Row paints is the most surreal picture of China I have read or heard told. The stories vary from foreigners working in Hong Kong to Chinese businessmen and their love lives. The opening story, *The Secret of Bats*, is about a teacher's student who tries to learn the art of echolocation. *The Train to Lo Wu*, while also being the title of the collection, is about a young Chinese man from Hong Kong who meets a girl from across the border in Shenzhen, a thriving Chinese megalopolis.

■ **Taipan by James Clavell**
Taipan is the story of a Scottish ship captain and his family set during the British occupation of Hong Kong. Like the rest of Clavell's Asia Saga, the story is a fictitious history. The characters visit Hong Kong, Guangzhou, and Macau as the lead character, Dirk Struan, seeks to be Tai Pan (king) of all of Hong Kong. This book, perhaps with the exception of Shogun, is the best Asia Saga book I have read. The book contains lots of action and is written from the point of view from many of the characters, both good and bad.

■ **Eating Smoke by Chris Thrall**
Chris Thrall, an ex-Royal Marine from England, gives a first hand account of his experience working as a doorman addicted to meth in Wan Chai, Hong Kong's red light district. The memoir reads quickly and his descriptions and observations are awesome. It's a humorous and interesting tale of one of the most vibrant places in the world.

■ **Wild Swans by Jung Chang**
Wild Swans is an account of the author's family living in Communist China during the rule of Mao Ze Dong. In particular the story revolves around Chang's grandmother who was born in the late 1800s, her mother, and herself. Much of the account takes place in Sichuan province where Chang is born and raised. The book covers an epic portion of modern Chinese history from the late 1800s to the late 1900s, and during the Nationalist party and Chiang Kai-shek's rule after Sun Yat-sen dies, the promise of greatness that Mao's Communist China will bring, and the Gang of Four's Cultural Revolution and the hells it unleashes on the Chinese people. As a Chinese modern history book, this is perfect.

▨ River Town by Peter Hessler

Peter Hessler taught English in China with the Peace Corps in the mid 1990s and was one of the first foreigners to live and work in Fuling, a small city that is now part of Chongqing province. *River Town* is the story of the two years he spent teaching in the city. Many foreign English teachers in China resonate strongly with his experience and most have had a very similar experience teaching in China, myself included. Friends of mine who have taught in other developing nations around the world have told me they resonated strongly with Hessler's story as well.

▨ The Man Who Loved China by Simon Winchester

The Man Who Loved China is a biography of Joseph Needham, a British scientist and historian, focused on China for much of his life after discovering its charms and mysteriousness.

"The Needham Question" is "Why did China not revolutionize faster than the West despite their early successes with technology?" and is the question that spurs Needham on for most of the book. He seeks to answer his questions in his history volumes: Science and Civilization in China.

FILMS

▨ Infernal Affairs

Technically this is a Hong Kong film, however, this is just a great movie. If you thought *The Departed* was good, this will be even better. It is the original movie that *The Departed* is a remake of. The film is directed by Andrew Lau and Alan Mak, and stars Tony Leung, Anthony Wong, Kelly Chen, Eric Tsang, and Andy Lau. Watch it!

▨ Chopstick Brothers' Films

The Chopstick Brothers are a two-person band, which comprises of Wang Taili and Xiao Yang. Xiao Yang is also a writer-director-actor and Wang Taili is an actor. Both of them have an excellent sense of humor, which comes through quite well in their music videos and short films.

Their most famous short film to date is *Lao Nan Hai*, meaning Old Boy. The story is about two men who enter a talent show and recall their high school days when they had also entered a talent show. The film spread through China's twenty and thirty year olds like wildfire as this generation resonated strongly with Chopstick Brothers' story about unrealized dreams.

Another two great short films are both called *Father*, the first film being about a father-daughter relationship and the second about father and son. Both contain high quality humor with strong story.

▓ Crouching Tiger Hidden Dragon

Ang Lee's *Crouching Tiger Hidden Dragon* is a film about warriors in the north of China. This film was nominated for Best Picture at the Oscars in 2000 as many people know, only to lose to *American Beauty* (also an excellent film).

▓ Hero

Qin Shi Huang is the first emperor of China and he is naturally a ruthless murderer. The audience slowly finds out that the story's protagonist has come to assassinate the emperor. The assassin tells the emperor a mix of stories full of mixed truths. Zhang Yimo directs the film, and Jet Li, Tony Leung, Donnie Yen, and Zhang Ziyi star in it.

▓ A Touch of Sin

A Touch of Sin is a 2013 film by Jia Zhangke and is a series of four stories set in modern China. The stories are loosely based on true events and are all violent. One who has spent time in China will feel the stories hit home and they paint a good picture of the desperation that has accompanied China's rapid rise in recent years. The film won Jia the 2013 Cannes Film Festival Best Screenplay award.

■ **Dreaming of Zhongshan** (www.vimeo.
com/129442903; http://v.youku.com/v_show/
id_XMTI1NjcxODYyNA)
A high quality short film about a young man's search for
romance and meaning in the surreal Zhongshan nights of
southern China. The film was written, produced, filmed,
and edited by my brother, our friends, and I.

CHAPTER 8

ARRIVAL IN CHINA AND SETTLING IN

GETTING AN APARTMENT

AS I'VE ALREADY MENTIONED, the school you work for will likely provide you with an apartment or a stipend for an apartment.

The Free Apartment

If you are teaching at a college, the college will likely provide you with an apartment on campus. Everyone I know who has taught English at a college in China has had this arrangement.

The first apartment I stayed at in China was of good quality. Though not huge, there was plenty of room for a single person. It had a living room, kitchen, bathroom, bedroom, and balcony. It was fully furnished with a TV, laundry machine, microwave, western toilet, and air conditioner. This is common.

Gas, electric, and water were all subsidized by the school and I usually only needed to pay around 100 RMB ($15) per month for utilities. If this were unsubsidized, this would be 150 RMB per month.

The Paid Apartment

Whether your school gives you a stipend or you select to live off campus in an apartment you select and pay for yourself, this section will explain the basics of what you will need to know.

In the downtown of a third-tier city like Zhongshan, an average, fully furnished two-bedroom apartment is about 1,400 RMB ($230) per month. Zhongshan is also a rather wealthy city in China. A high-end two-bedroom apartment in China in a small city like this might cost 3,000 RMB ($500) per month. In a big city like Beijing or Shanghai, it might cost 3,000 RMB for a small one-bedroom apartment on the outskirts of the city center.

While living in Jiaxing, during my later years in China, I was not fortunate enough to have an apartment paid for by my employer. I relied on an agency to show me different apartments throughout the city and also contacted agents through apartment rental websites. When apartment hunting like this, it is best to have a Chinese speaker helping you because the websites will not be in English and the agents may not speak English.

An agency's fee is an entire month's rent. In Jiaxing, in 2012, I ended up finding a brand new, high-end studio apartment on the edge of the city close to the factory office I worked at for 1,500 RMB ($250) per month.

- **Apartments in Shanghai** (www.apartmentinshanghai.com)
  A website catering to foreigners looking for apartments in Shanghai.

- **Beijing** (www.bj.58.com)
  A website for finding apartments in Beijing.

■ **Jiaxing** (www.jx.58.com)
A website for finding apartments in Jiaxing.

■ **Zhongshan** (www.zs.58.com)
A website for finding apartments in Zhongshan.

Getting a Residence Permit

Once you obtain a Z visa, which is usually only good for 30 days and one or two entries, you will need to exchange it at the bureau of foreign affairs in the city you will be living in, in order to acquire a resident permit. The resident permit is multi-entry and good for one year or until you break contract with your employer.

When you arrive in China, within the first week or two, someone with your employer will take you to the bureau of foreign affairs in order to begin the process of exchanging your work visa for a residence permit. Before going to the bureau of foreign affairs with your passport, you will probably need to go to a Chinese clinic for a check up (even if you already did one back home for the work visa), as well as get passport photos, which are of the correct size for China. Once this has been done, you will need to wait a week or two while your passport is being processed. Once this is finished you will have a residence permit good for one year. If you are still with your employer a year later, it will not be difficult to renew. You may need to go through the same process, but you won't need to do everything you originally did for your work visa.

FURNISHINGS AND SHOPPING

As I just mentioned in the previous section, apartments in China are usually furnished and there is usually little need to buy your own furniture. However, the beds are rock-hard without exception, so many foreigners opt to go to Ikea to purchase a mattress or more comfortable sofa. This will cost you though as the prices are usually a little higher than in North America for such things. An Ikea can be found in the largest city of most provinces. Usually a sleek, high-speed train can take you there. The delivery system is also fairly efficient. Even if you can't write the address in Chinese, the deliverymen will usually find your apartment somehow.

In addition to furnishings, there will naturally be many other supplies you will need. Fortunately (or unfortunately), it seems like there is a giant mall on every other block in China and you will probably not need to go far before finding a supermarket that sells everything you need. Here, you will be able to buy cleaning supplies, soap, towels, cooking utensils, clothes, rugs, mirrors, locks, and more.

Besides malls, there are also markets where vendors are lined up in shops next to each other or sometimes out in open-air stalls. You will find all of the same products at these types of places and the price (and oftentimes quality) will be lower than in the supermarket.

UTILITIES

The main Internet providers in China are China Telecom, China Mobile, and China Unicom. All are fine. For some firewalled Internet goodness it will cost you about 70 to 120 RMB per month.

You will probably be cooking with a gas burner and may use gas to heat your shower water. If your apartment does not have a gas line coming into it, gas will be delivered by gas companies via motorbike drivers that carry two cans of it each, one on either side of their motorbike. Your school or landlord will be able to connect you up with such companies. You will need to call and have your gas replaced when it runs out, but this will probably only be once per year or less, depending on how much you use it.

Alternatively, if your apartment does have a gas line your

landlord may give you a card, which you then charge at a bank or management office in order to get more gas. Water is cheap and will only cost about five to 10 RMB per month per person. It should be noted that you should not drink the sink water in China unless you want to get sick. For drinking water, you will need to order tanks of it, which can then be dispensed by a water disperser, a common technology in everyone's home.

BANKING IN CHINA

China is a cash culture. Almost everything is paid for in cash, including apartments and cars sometimes. The concept of credit cards and debit cards is catching on increasingly each year though.

With almost all of the teaching jobs I have had in China, I have been paid in cash. For the first three years I taught at the college in Zhongshan, at the start of every month I would go to an office with my fellow foreign teacher colleagues and get paid about 6,000 *yuan* in cash.

Although you may be paid in cash, you will still want to set up a bank account. Someone at your school will probably take you to the bank the first time you are paid in order to open an account and deposit your money. Almost nothing is needed other than a passport to open a bank account.

Once you have your account, you will be given a bankcard, which will probably have something called Union Pay, which is a like a debit card. You can withdraw money from ATMs around China and also make payments with the card at many restaurants and other establishments

Some banks I have used in China include China Construction Bank and Bank of China. Both are fine, and many of the other banks around the city are probably fine. A bank like HSBC may also be good because they have banks all over the world (unlike Bank of China and China

Construction Bank). However, HSBC usually only has locations in larger cities.

Wiring Money

At some point, you may wire money back home. This is completely doable, but may be a pain. For some reason, foreigners are not allowed to easily transfer money in China. Because of this, you will need a Chinese person to help you deposit money into their account and then send the money to your home account. Use a trusted friend or colleague.

In addition to the account name and number, you will need a SWIFT code (a type of code used to identify banks) and the address of your local bank back home. The exchange rate the banks use is accurate and they won't charge you much extra besides a wiring fee, whereas many moneychangers will have a percentage they take. Without using a Chinese friend to wire money, the most you will be able to wire per transaction is $500.

PHONE

I was surprised when I moved back to the United States from China in 2013 to see people still texting to each other. I hadn't sent more than five text messages in China for the last year and a half. The phone application, WeChat, similar to WhatsApp, has taken over China the way Facebook took over the United States a decade ago.

WeChat allows its users to send text messages and voice messages over the Internet. It also allows users to call one another (much like Skype videophone and Google Hangouts), take and send photographs, and a lot more.

In this section I'll be sharing tactics on how to get set up with a phone so you too can take advantage of this Chinese app as well as make calls the normal way.

Finding a Phone

If you don't have a phone that you can use in China, you will need to purchase one. There is usually a cell phone district within each city so you may find phones there. There are Apple Stores (both real and fake, so judge wisely), and many malls that sell cell phones. People in China will save a month to a year's worth of their salary to buy an iPhone sometimes. Other options include Samsung, HTC, Xiaomi, Huawei and Nokia. Some cheaper options include Nokia and Xiaomi. Xiaomi is a cheap Chinese phone of good quality.

SIM Cards

In China, most people use pay-as-you-go plans and recharge their SIM cards every few months at mobile phone service providers. Typically I would use my phone a normal amount, making and receiving several local calls a day and end up paying around 100 RMB ($15) per month. New SIM cards and activation are free.

There are two main providers of cell phone service in China: China Mobile and China Unicom. I have used both and do not have a preference. Both are not very expensive if you are making a decent salary (6,000 RMB or $1,000 is considered great by Chinese standards and is usually the minimum a foreigner would be paid for a job in China). Both provide data, minutes, texting packages, and every day it is getting cheaper and the standards are becoming better. Bring your passport and a Chinese friend when getting a SIM card.

Always be on the look out for different convenience stores that double as places to recharge your phone. Ask if they provide this service. If they do, write down your phone number and give them the amount you would like added and they will add it. You will get a text message when the money has been added to your account.

In addition to charging up your phone at convenience stores, WeChat has a function called WeChat Wallet, which allows a person to charge up their phone through adding money to their Wallet from their bank account and then put more money on their phone. You can also send money to your friends using this same function. There is a similar app in the West called Venmo.

Calling Home

The main issue with calling home is the time difference. Depending on where home is, there will probably only be a few hours at the beginning or end of the day where the time zones align, and both parties can speak.

Figure out how many hours apart you are from where you are trying to call before applying the following tactics. Unless you don't mind people calling you in the middle of the night or making such calls yourself.

There are a lot of cheap options available, so you shouldn't be too quick to just use your phone to call internationally and spend $20 on a two-minute call. My go-to software for calling home has always been Skype. China has banned the authentic version of it for some reason, but you should still be able to use their other version, which works the same way with your account. If you can't arrange for the other party to be online at the same time, you will need to call their cell phone. This can be done by adding $10 to your account and then calling their cell phone for $0.02/ min. The connection can sometimes have issues and you may need to hang up and dial again, but it is usually pretty reliable.

If your family and friends are tech savvy, they can do the same thing and call you on your cell phone from Skype. You may also use your smart phone to do this, so it is like talking from phone to phone, but it uses up battery power fast.

The best option though is WeChat. The problem with this is that your friends may not want to download one app just to talk with you. My friends and family and I usually ended up scheduling Skype or Google Hangout chats.

WeChat is great because it has the videophone or phone function and you can use it to call phone to phone for free. It is available in English.

THE CHINESE INTERNET

Getting Internet Service

After you have a phone and are connected with service, you will probably want to set up Internet at your apartment. As with Internet service providers in the United States and elsewhere in the world, this process can take a few days, but unlike services like Century Link or Comcast, it is not a painful process.

Take your passport and go to either China Unicom, China Mobile, or China Telecom. Take a numbered ticket, which a nearby security guard will usually be able to help you with if you don't know what to do. Decent speeds will cost you 70-120 RMB per month and this is usually paid in a lump sum of half a year.

Within a few business days, someone will come to your apartment to set up your Internet connection. You may need to purchase a modem from them for 100-200 RMB. I also usually invest in my own wireless router if their modem does not include this.

Now that you are all set up with Internet and phones, we are ready to explore what they can do.

VPNs and Blocked Websites

It is probably common knowledge around the world at this point that the Chinese government blocks sites like You-Tube, Facebook, and Twitter. Google sites such as Google

Drive, Google Hangouts, and Gmail are also blocked now. For the full list of which websites are blocked visit this webpage: https://en.wikipedia.org/wiki/Websites_blocked_in_ mainland_China. The sites that are blocked sometimes become unblocked for periods of time.

A solution to this issue though is getting a VPN (Virtual Private Network). Once this is set up you will be able to visit basically any site that is blocked in China. For more on VPNs, go here: www.bestvpninchina.com. VPNs can usually be purchased, downloaded, and installed for $60 per year.

In addition to browsing websites that are blocked, you should check out some of these websites.

- **Baidu** (www.baidu.com)

Baidu is the Google of China and it serves as a good search engine if you are searching for anything in Chinese.

Since Google Maps is now blocked in China, a better option may be using Baidu Maps, which is a good alternative for looking at where things are located in China and getting directions. Everything will be in Chinese though.

Baidu Music allows you to download many Chinese and foreign music for free, much like Napster back in the day. There is also probably something like Baidu Docs, which could be good for collaborating.

- **QQ** (http://blog.imqq.com/download/)

QQ is one of the most popular websites in China. It is also the premier instant messaging platform. There is an international version available and it is worth getting for speaking with friends on your computer or on your phone. It has some of the functionality of WeChat and both are owned by the same company, Tencent.

QQ Zone is like Facebook in that users can post pictures, leave messages for each other, and have a profile.

QQ Music is like Baidu Music.

- **PP Stream** (www.pps.tv/en/)
  Great name!
  PP Stream and the application, PPTV, can be used to stream TV shows and movies. Most TV shows and movies are Chinese, but there are also many foreign shows. The shows are on a rotation, much like the free shows on Hulu. Many of my former students used PPTV and PP Stream to watch foreign TV shows and improve their English.

- **iQIYI** (www.iqiyi.com)
  A website for watching movies.

- **AcFun** (www.acfun.tv)
  A website for viewing movies.

- **RenRen** (www.renren.com)
  RenRen is like the Facebook of China and similar to QQ Zone.

- **Weibo** (www.weibo.com)
  Weibo is the Twitter of China. Before WeChat, Weibo was the biggest craze and everyone was posting things on Weibo. Now WeChat seems to have usurped it. *Weibo* literally means "micro blog" and there are actually many different *weibo* platforms in China. The most ubiquitous is Sina Weibo and is the one I am referring to here.

- **Youku** (www.youku.com) **and Tudou** (www.tudou. com)
  Youku and Tudou are the YouTube's of China. These sites function the same way YouTube does and there are now many Chinese and foreign TV shows making their way onto them.

- **E-Commerce: Taobao** (www.taobao.com), **Jing Dong** (www.jd.com), **and TMall** (www.tmall.com)
  China dwarfs the United States in terms of online shopping. Many Chinese are avid online shoppers and Tabobao,

Jing Dong, and TMall are the three biggest online shopping portals. There is also Amazon.cn.

One may need a Chinese bank account to get set up properly first, before being able to buy anything. See the previous section on banking in China.

■ **Alibaba** (www.alibaba.com)

Alibaba is like Amazon but it is for business-to-business transactions. No matter what it is you are looking to make, from airplanes to ladders, there is a manufacturer on Alibaba that can make it. As the factory of the world, many of these factories are located in China.

■ **Grabtalk** (http://grabtalk.com)

For people whose Mandarin is not yet at the level for getting around and making reservations, this app is very useful. It allows one to connect with a bilingual person and have them help with reservations, buying products online, calling taxis, booking train tickets, etc.

Where to Find English (and Other Foreign Language) Books in China

A common problem in China used to be getting English books while living in cities where English is seldom spoken. Bookstores in bigger cities will have a collection of English books and some cities like Shanghai and Beijing will even have full on foreign bookstores, holding mainly English books.

However, now with devices such as Kindles, smart phones, and tablet computers, all one needs is an Internet connection to buy and download a book.

CHINESE POSTAL SERVICE

A postcard from my friend in Europe—how sweet. I looked at how it had been addressed. All that was written was the city name, Zhongshan, and my name. The mail delivery service can be impressive in China. Or maybe I should have been scared that they only needed my name to know where I lived in the city.

You may get some mail while you are in China. If you work and live at a school, the school will likely inform you when you have mail and at that point will be able to pick it up at the school or post office. If you order something online from Taobao, Jingdong, or Tmall, Chinese online E-commerce websites, you will get a call on your cellphone when the driver-postman is nearing or at your apartment. Although this system seems very sloppy, it is actually efficient. If you are busy they will probably leave it at the post office. Be sure to bring your passport to pick up your package.

INSURANCE

Medical insurance will be one of the benefits you receive from your school if you are working full time. You may not get dental insurance, but you will get medical insurance. Below are brief descriptions of what a hospital visit and dental clinic visit might look like.

Medical Clinics and Hospitals

For serious or even life threatening aliments, I recommend making an appointment with a Hong Kong clinic or hospital. For less serious maladies like broken bone, a cold, or flu, Chinese hospitals and clinics are usually fine. Just make sure it is a nice hospital and not the neighborhood clinic (though these too could be okay, I just have never been to one). If someone is sitting outside with an IV drip in his or her arm, this is the type of clinic I am talking about.

Please note, I am not a doctor and this is not medical advice.

Your school's insurance will pay for your medical needs in China, but you may need to pay for medicine on your own.

Dental Clinics

As a kid, I used to wear braces and I still have three fake teeth, so my experience with dentist visits in the United States is extensive. In China the quality of work may be a little lower than in your home country. However, for normal things like cleanings, they are fine.

I had some of my fake teeth come out while in China once. They aren't meant to stay glued in forever and so they need to be glued back in every few years. The Chinese dentist I visited tried to glue them back in, but they came out again after a week.

Finally, for a few hundred RMB, the dentist was able to make a small set of new fake teeth that I could slide into my mouth and would stay in. Though not as comfortable, this was a decent alternative and my problem was solved.

The cost of visiting the dentist is not very high. If you need serious work done, I would recommend going to Hong Kong and having your appointment coincide with a visit to the city.

Resources

As I mentioned before, if you have a serious problem I would seek treatment in Hong Kong or even fly back to your home country. If you are from the United States, fortunately there is great insurance that you can purchase from Seven Corners (www2.sevencorners.com) to cover these medical costs outside of mainland China. Look at their Reside Worldwide and Reside Prime plans.

This insurance is low-cost and lets you receive treatment from a first world country as long as you are not living in the United States for more than six months per year.

If you are not from United States, be sure to look online or ask around to see if similar insurance is available in your country.

CHAPTER 9

LEARNING MANDARIN CHINESE

HOW TO LEARN A LANGUAGE

THE FOLLOWING SECTION WILL give you a brief overview on how to learn Mandarin Chinese, the language with the most native speakers in the world, and the lingua franca of China. It is not meant to be a textbook, but instead a guide. After covering how to go about learning Mandarin effectively and enjoyably, I will provide a learning plan at the end of the section for you to follow.

Learning to speak Mandarin is not difficult, but it does take a long time to get good at it. The main question to ask yourself will be: how much is it worth to you? For some people becoming proficient at getting around is all that is needed. Others will want to become conversationally fluent in the language (meaning they can have simple conversations with relative ease). Whichever route you choose, by spending time learning the words that will be most helpful to you in your daily life, you will be surprised at how much you can learn in the course of a few months to a year.

In my opinion, the most important part to living well in China is connecting with the Chinese people in their native language. This is the most enjoyable part of living in China, and it will also make your life tremendously easier because you will be able to get around easily without needing to rely on others who speak Mandarin better than you do.

Some people may view learning languages as difficult because they arrive in a country with little experience speaking with natives in their own tongue and then think of themselves as bad at languages. On the other hand, a person may think they know a lot of a given language from what they learned in school, but when it comes to using the language in a country where the language is spoken they find that they can't communicate because everything they learned was from a textbook and they had no practice speaking and listening to the language in the field. Everyone sounds terrible the first time they speak a foreign language with a native speaker. The key is to keep doing it and learn from mistakes. There will be many mistakes.

The fastest, most enjoyable, and most interesting way I have found to learn a language is to speak it with people everyday, and find things your are curious about and want to understand, to use as motivation for language learning. Usually when you are feeling curious, you will learn a lot and it won't feel so difficult. It is because of this that for most of the rest of this guide, I will include tips for learning Mandarin as I go along.

Curiosity is the best teacher there is. Develop curiosity about people and don't be intimidated to learn about topics that are of interest to you, but may seem not very useful (learning about photography in Mandarin for example). When you begin, it doesn't matter if what you learn is useful or not. Be curious about something and that curiosity will carry you through and you will learn many things that you never even thought about that end up being tremendously valuable (learning Mandarin grammar from reading about photography for example).

LANGUAGES OF CHINA

Like the people of Europe, the people of China all speak different languages. Each province is like a different country in this regard. Some people call the different languages of China dialects and though there are also many dialects in China, what I am referring to here as languages are mutually unintelligible means of communication. A person who only speaks Mandarin will not understand Cantonese or Shanghainese, and a person who only speaks Taiwanese will not understand Cantonese or Mandarin, and so on.

The common language of China is Mandarin and this is the language we will be looking at in this guide. Other common languages include Cantonese, which is spoken mostly in Guangdong and Hong Kong, Taiwanese, which is spoken in Fujian and Taiwan, Shanghainese, which is spoken in Shanghai, Hakka, which is spoken in and around Guangdong, Gan, which is spoken in Jiangxi, and Tibetan, which is spoken in Tibet, to name a few.

When choosing where to live in China you might want to take into account how predominant a given language is. Mandarin comes from the north of China, and it's here that it is spoken in a standard way. I learned Mandarin while living in Guangdong primarily and although it is sometimes frustrating trying to decipher what people are saying when using incorrect pronunciation, I found that the majority of people still understood me and that I could understand them as well. It also made me better at hearing the language spoken in many different ways.

PINYIN

When people hear the word "Mandarin Chinese" they may think of incoherent scribbles.

"You can read all those sticks?" an Indian woman remarked to my brother and I at a restaurant in Goa, India.

I advise people who are first learning Mandarin to hold off on learning characters for a while until they get better at listening and speaking. When you do start learning Chinese you will need some way to write down what you are learning, and therefore you are going to need to learn *pinyin*.

Pinyin is the Romanization of Chinese characters. This means that an alphabet is used to represent the sounds of the characters. Learning this alphabet is very straightforward, and there are no surprises like with English spellings. One thing you will quickly notice is that there are very few sounds in Mandarin. Many of the words sound similar to an untrained ear. With time and repetition you will be able to hear the differences. Just know that learning *pinyin* is very important and will help with not only learning Mandarin, but even once you attain fluency, you will still use it when learning new words, typing, and more.

For interactive *pinyin* tables with audio, search for the words "pinyin table" online and you will find many resources. Print out a guide like this and have it nearby at all times in the beginning. Listen to the sounds and repeat them over and over until you start to remember them and can start hearing them when people say the sounds on the street. Don't worry if you don't know what they mean yet, the goal is just to become familiar with the sounds of the language.

LISTENING AND SPEAKING

Even before beginning to learn pinyin, start listening to Mandarin, as this is the first step towards speaking the language. I will provide some of the resources I use for listening at the end of this Chapter, but for now, know that listening is the most important thing when just starting to learn a language.

Once you hear a word or a phrase, you should try repeating it—knowing the meaning is not so important at this point. Doing so repeatedly will make you more and more familiar with the sounds of the language. At the same time, study the alphabet and *pinyin* table in order to start learning the correct pronunciation of words. Pronunciation is very important and should be addressed at the very beginning, especially because Mandarin uses so few sounds compared with English. Having a teacher to help correct pronunciation is also important.

Tones

When learning Mandarin, many people become intimidated by the tones because their native language does not have tones and they can't hear the difference between four words that sound the same, but have different tones. I admit this can take some time to learn and it took me two years before I could distinguish between all four tones without any trouble, particularly the second and third tones. However, this process of adjustment does not need to be difficult. Go easy on yourself and be patient, and with time you will start hearing the differences. The first and fourth tones are not as difficult to distinguish from the others in my opinion.

Although you may not think your native English uses tones, it actually might. Most languages do use tones, it's just that we don't think about it. In English, at the end of a question, one typically raises their voice on the last word. However, if the sentence is not a question, there will be no raising of the voice on the last word. Compare the two sentences below.

Do you want some pretzels?

These pretzels are making me thirsty.

The top sentence has a rising tone at the end, while the second has none.

There are four tones in Mandarin. The first tone is a high flat tone as in "do", "re", or "mi". The second tone is a rising tone as is used at the end of a question in many languages. The third tone falls and then rises, and is similar to the second tone. The fourth tone is a falling tone. Think about a parent scolding a child: "Put that down!" The word "down" starts high and finishes low.

Speaking Mandarin

As I mentioned earlier, I believe that the best way to learn a language is to use it. China is a great place to learn a foreign language because so many of the people are open to helping you learn it, no matter your level. This doesn't mean that they will point out mistakes, it just means that they will give you the practice you are looking for.

As for which phrases to focus on learning first, these should be the phrases you will encounter in every day life and need to listen for and answer the most. Many phrases will be those referring to yourself. In the next section, I will cover a common situation in China, which is also an ideal way to learn Mandarin: a ride with a taxi cab driver. The section will contain useful vocabulary and phrases. Throughout the rest of the book I will point out key phrases to learn for a given common situation.

Below, I illustrate how speaking Mandarin is incorporated into daily life. Effectively using Mandarin to help you get around is a huge confidence booster. With each little language victory you make, you will gain confidence in the language and in your learning abilities. I encourage you to learn some of the below phrases first when learning Mandarin as they will be common and useful.

A Taxi Ride

It is a beautiful sunny day in Zhongshan and I'm meeting some friends at an Indian restaurant for lunch. I walk downstairs from my apartment, hail a cab, and get in. The driver starts up a conversation with me.

Driver: *Ni shi nali ren?* Where are you from?

You will hear this phrase daily and it will be one of the first sentences you pick up that others are asking you.

Nick: *Wo shi meiguo ren.* I'm American.

Replace the country with the country you are from and that is how you tell someone where you are from.

Driver: *Meiguo ren hen hao a!* Americans are great!

Driver: *Nide gongzuo shi shenme?* What's your job?

As when meeting anyone new, Chinese or not, this is a common question to be asked.

Nick: *Wo shi laoshi.* I'm a teacher.

Since you will probably be teaching English if you are reading this guide, it's likely that this will be a useful phrase.

Driver: *Gongzi shi duoshao qian?* How much money do you make?

It's common to be asked this question early on in some relationships in China. The cab drivers and shopkeepers I meet are always quick to ask me this question anyway.

Nick: *Liuqian wu.* Six thousand five hundred.

When answering this question, it is assumed they are asking about the monthly salary. Cab driver's usually make around two thousand or three thousand RMB per month.

Driver: *Ni jiehun le ma?* Are you married?

As with most cultures, the topic of mating is typically the most interesting to the most people and I like how the Chinese cab drivers get straight to it.

Nick: *Mei you.* No.

Instead of directly saying "No" as in "I am not", *mei you* means "have not" as in "I have not yet married." In Mandarin this phrase is used a lot.

Driver: *Na ni you nvpengyou ma?* Then do you have a girlfriend?

Nick: *Ye mei you.* I also don't.

Driver: *Ni yinggai zhao yige zhongguo lao po.* You should find a Chinese wife.

The above conversation comes up repeatedly in China when meeting new people. Learning the phrases that you will use in everyday conversations are the ones to learn first.

Some Grammar
When telling someone "I am a teacher" or some other profession or characteristic, you will usually use the word "*shi*" which means "am" or "to be" in most situations. Examples of this can be seen in the previous conversation.

Wo shi meiguo ren. I'm American.

Wo shi laoshi. I'm a teacher.

However, when describing someone with an adjective like in, "You are very great" there often is no "to be" verb and instead one directly says "*Ni hen hao*" or "You very good" literally.

Meiguo ren hen hao a! Americans are great!

When learning a language, many people psyche themselves out in the field. They've been learning common phrases for six months, but they are startled by the fact that the other person is speaking a foreign language and they don't realize they've probably already learned the phrases the other person is saying. Don't be that person! Listen closely and tell yourself that you've probably encountered the phrases the other person is speaking. It's sort of like magic, if you think you can understand it, you starting picking up on things and slowly realize that you actually do understand it. This takes time and you won't know everything that the other person is saying, but you do probably know more than you think you do.

READING AND WRITING

"Hey Dean, what are these characters I keep seeing over and over again?" I asked my new friend, Dean, the leader and organizer of a group of students that volunteered to help foreign teachers with their transition to life in Zhongshan, China. The characters were much simpler than the others, so were easy to pick out: "中山".

"That's 'Zhongshan' man, the name of this city. 'Zhong' means middle, and 'shan' means mountain," he said.

I'd learned the character "zhong" before coming to China while learning the phrase "Ta shi zhongguo ren" or "She is Chinese." The sound at the beginning of the word "Chinese" meant "China" or literally "Middle Country" as in the Middle Kingdom. This same character was used in the name of the city I lived in, and now I knew what it looked like. As a square with a line down the middle, it did sort of depict the idea of "middle." "Shan" had three spikes pointing upwards and resembled three mountain peaks. Initially I had assumed it was impossible for a foreigner to learn Chinese characters, but having learned two simple characters relatively easily, I thought it might be possible to learn a few more.

The simple characters on billboards, signs, and menus

stood out to me and I began to learn them. "人" (*ren*) meant "people," "一" (*yi*) meant "one," "大" (*da*) meant "big," "中" (*zhong*) meant "middle," "山" (*shan*) meant "mountain," "女" (*nv*) meant "woman," and "子" (*zi*) meant "child." Although I still had no idea what I was reading most of the time, since most Chinese words are comprised of two or three characters, I could understand and say (with terrible pronunciation and tones) at least half of the words that contained such simple characters.

Chinese Characters

As I'm sure you're aware by now, Mandarin does not use an alphabet. Instead it uses thousands of little pictures called characters for words. Each word is usually made of two or three characters and it's necessary to learn somewhere around three thousand in order to read a newspaper. However, simply learning a character is not enough. It is the thousands of words and phrases that these characters produce that must be learned in order to read a newspaper.

For example, the character "定" (*ding*) means "certain" and the character "一" (*yi*) means "one." While "*yi*" may be used by itself in many situations, "*ding*" is typically not used alone. The word "一定" (*yiding*) means "certainly" but simply learning the meaning of the characters *yi* and *ding* separately does not mean that one will know that *yiding* means "certainly." Furthermore, Mandarin does not uses spaces between words so it's very hard to determine where one word ends, and another begins unless you have previously learned those words and sentence structures.

It is for these reasons that I recommend shying away from learning characters at the start of your Mandarin studies. As your listening and speaking improve, you may want to start learning characters for common vocabulary, place names, and food names.

I mentioned before that many Chinese languages are

spoken in China. To make things a little easier, they all use the same Chinese characters, but have different sounds in different languages. There is both a written language and a spoken language. The spoken language in these other languages might be depicted with other characters that a Mandarin speaker would not typically use when writing. We won't touch on these, but just know that languages like Cantonese and Shanghainese use additional characters purely for their sounds.

When learning characters, stick to the vocabulary you already know and learn those characters first. If you keep seeing a particular character somewhere, like on a menu or a display in a store, take a picture or copy it down and ask your teacher what it means the next time you see him or her.

Radicals

After a few weeks in our new home, my fellow foreign teachers and I were given free Chinese classes courtesy of the college we worked at.

A lot of what we learned was sometimes hard to keep up with and as with most language classes taught to groups larger than one to two people, eighty to ninety percent of the material was forgotten ten minutes after class or never picked up in the first place.

Things I did remember learning though were a few new characters. One new character was "好" (hao). "Hao" meant "good". There was something interesting about this character though. It looked like it was made up of two simpler characters I had learned before: "女" (nv) and "子" (zi). A few seconds later and I would have my assumptions confirmed.

"This character is made up of two smaller characters. We call these radicals. Here "nv" means "woman" and "zi" means "child". And in Chinese thought we think that a woman being with her child is good. So this character means 'good,'" our teacher said.

As with "好" (hao) I would soon start to pick out other characters where I recognized all of the radicals. "林" (lin) was another, which meant "forest" and was made up of two "木" (mu), which meant "wood."

Learning Characters

After you begin to learn many of the simple characters, you will start to see that many characters are made up of two or three of these simple characters, even though they will sometimes look elongated or smushed.

Learning these characters next is logical. Almost every character in Chinese is made up a few different radicals. There are two hundred and fourteen of these radicals. Some of them will be exactly the same as what they are when alone, others will be adapted to the character and not look like the simple character they are when by themselves.

If you do decide to start learning to read characters, one of the best ways to go about doing this is to read children's stories. Have a dictionary handy because you will need it constantly.

CONJUNCTIONS

Many foreigners have been in China for years and can't speak the language. But what I've found is that they actually know many of the vocabulary words they need in order to communicate. They may be daunted when they hear Chinese rapidly coming out of a shop owner's mouth, but they likely know more of the language than they think.

Their problem is that they don't know how to put the phrases together. This is because they primarily know the nouns and adjectives, but not many of the verbs and conjunctions. After learning some key nouns, verbs, and adjectives, as well as some basic grammar, learning the be-low conjunctions will help you with sentence creation.

Some key conjunctions in Mandarin are "*suoyi*" (所以) meaning "so" or "therefore," "*ranhou*" (然后) meaning "and then," "*he*" (和) meaning "and," "*xiang*" (像) meaning "like," "*ruguo*" (如果) meaning "if," "*huozhe*" (或者) mean-ing "or," "*yinwei*" (因为) meaning "because," and "*danshi*" (但是) meaning "but".

Use these conjunctions to make more complex state-ments and tell longer stories.

RESOURCES
Below are some of the resources I have used when learning Chinese as well as others that may be worth checking out. They are organized by type of material: listening, reading, and applications.

■ **Chinese Learn Online** (www.chineselearnonline.com)
For those interested in listening to the right sentenc-es and words from the beginning and then building from that, this is the best tool I have found. This online course consists of dialogues with audio episodes and transcripts. Each level builds upon the one before and constant review is built right in.

■ **Chinese Pod** (www.chinesepod.com)
Chinese Pod is a series of audio episodes teaching Man-darin through short dialogues from real life situations in China. The background information can be interesting for someone looking to learn more about modern China and the content is good. The only problem is that they jump around a lot so it might be frustrating for the first time learner to not be reviewing certain words every day when really one should be.

■ **Yoyo Chinese** (www.yoyochinese.com)
Video lessons taught by the Chinese teacher and

television host, Yang Yang. I have not used this course but the demos I have watched seem very suitable for a beginner.

- **Pimsleur Chinese** (www.pimsleur.com/ Learn-Chinese-Mandarin)

The Pimsleur method is based on timed repetition of phrases that are spaced out just right to increase memory connections. Each phrase is repeated right around the time you are likely to forget it so that you will remember a particular phrase for longer and longer. There is a lot of repetition of similar phrases in order to help you remember the phrases. It's thanks to Pimsleur that I still know how to say "I'm an American" in five languages, even though all I have done is listen to one Pimsleur CD with some of them. I can't emphasize the importance of listening enough when learning a new language. You can buy this online or borrow it from a friend.

- **FSI Language Courses** (www.fsi-language-courses. net/)

If you are good enough to land a job with the US Foreign Service and be paid to use this material, that's awesome. You can use this if you don't have such a job.

Phrasebooks

Mandarin phrasebooks are a great source for learning grammar and relevant Mandarin words. Many of them have a dictionary that includes the most common words. Some names include *Lonely Planet*, *Berlitz*, and *At a Glance*. *At a Glance* was my first "textbook" and I got a lot of mileage out if it. Phrasebooks are especially good for learning *pinyin* and basic grammar.

- **Integrated Chinese** (www.amzn.to/1z0DvuU)

This textbook is used by universities all over the United

States and makes a great beginning textbook. There is also an accompanying workbook for each level.

■ **Boya Chinese** (www.amzn.to/1zxg4MT)
Chinese universities use this textbook for teaching foreigners Mandarin and while it is a good resource for advanced learners, it might not be the most intuitive book, which can make learning slow when first starting. There are more than a dozen books and levels. I started using this series after learning Mandarin for three years.

■ **WeChat** (www.wechat.com/en/)
Although I really stress listening, actually using the language would be a close second when first starting and quickly becomes the most important once you get better. Messaging apps and texting are some of the best ways to communicate with others.

This is the most popular phone-messaging app in China. I never text with friends in China anymore, I only use this. It's like Facebook on your phone and everyone has it. While speaking with people is good practice when first starting out, it can be difficult to understand what the other person is saying. In a face-to-face interaction you won't have much time to react unless the other person is very patient. Texting back and forth is valuable because it gives you time to figure out what the other person is saying and time to construct the perfect response.

When first meeting a person, get their WeChat. Then later you can message with them as much as you want without scaring them away. You can copy and paste what they say into the electronic dictionary Pleco (see below) in order to translate and learn. This is a very effective way of learning.

- **Momo** (www.immomo.com/?v=en)
- **Badoo** (https://badoo.com)
- **Tinder** (www.gotinder.com)
- **Skout** (www.skout.com)
- **Tantan** (tantanapp.com)

The above apps are dating apps you can use to meet other people and then practice Mandarin by messaging with them.

- **QQ** (http://blog.imqq.com/download/)

This is the most popular instant messaging app in China. Many people in China do not have email and some companies just use QQ to communicate. You can get this on your computer and phone.

- **Memrise** (www.memrise.com)

Use this website to memorize new characters and words. There are numerous decks made by people in order of most common characters to least common.

- **MDBG** (www.mdbg.net)

MDBG is an online dictionary for learning Chinese characters and words.

- **Yellow Bridge** (www.yellowbridge.com)

Yellow Bridge is another online dictionary, and it also has a tool that shows the etymology of each character. In other words, it explains the meaning of the character based on the radicals that comprise it.

- **HanziCraft** (www.hanzicraft.com)

HanziCraft is another online dictionary.

- **Lang-8** (http://lang-8.com)

This website allows users to post sentences in the language they are trying to learn and get corrections and feedback from native speakers. This is very useful for checking whether the sentences you are forming are being formed correctly.

■ **Pleco** (www.pleco.com)

I saved the best for last. If you could only have one resource listed here, this would be it. This electronic dictionary, which is compatible with most smart phones will be a valuable asset when in China as you navigate business and social settings. I use it daily no matter where I am in the world.

STUDY PLAN

Now that you have a basic idea of what learning Mandarin consists of and some resources for learning it, I want to give you a brief study plan for effectively learning Mandarin. I'll go over listening, speaking, reading, and writing, as well as give general tips for learning.

Find a good resource or resources to listen to and start repeating what is said. I recommend trying a few different things to see what works best for you. Pimsleur, Yoyo Chinese, Chinese Pod, and Chinese Learn Online are all good options. I used Pimsleur.

Get a grammar book and start looking through it. Pay special attention to the beginning of the book, which will probably have a *pinyin* table, basic grammar, and table of tones. Go online and find a *pinyin* table that allows you to listen to how each sound is said when you click on it. Spend three weeks doing these two tasks for thirty minutes a day and you will have completed the basic groundwork for learning Mandarin. This will mostly be review of the same material again and again until it makes sense.

Find a teacher and have them write down common words and phrases you would like to know in *pinyin*. Phrases could include: "How much is this?", "I want this one," "I'm a teacher," "Thank you," and "No."

Practice using your phrases with other people: taxi drivers, shop owners, waitresses, security guards, etc. This is when the key learning will happen and when you will gain the confidence to realize that it's actually possible to learn enough Mandarin to get around if you go about learning the right way. Experiment with new phrases by substituting in and out different words. Instead of saying, "I like noodles," trying asking "Do you like noodles?" using only the words you already know. If you've studied enough basic grammar and are comfortable with these simple words, you will probably know how to formulate this new sentence and be understood.

Once you feel comfortable with basic listening and speaking, it's okay to start learning some key characters. Start by learning the simple-looking characters as you will have already learned their pronunciation and meaning. Many of these characters are also radicals, so you will now know the characters that make up more complex characters. From here, you will be ready to start learning place names and food names. If you have not already asked your teacher how to say the place names and food names that are most useful to you, do so now. These are the characters that will be most useful to learn since you will need to keep an eye out for them at train stations, airports, bus stations, and restaurants.

With your dictionary and teacher as guides, start reading a short children's book. The simpler the better at this point. If there is a book made for a three-year-old, get that. Write down the pronunciations of characters you don't know while going through the book sentence by sentence. Go back and review often.

Finally, the most useful and effective way of learning Mandarin will be texting with other people. Download WeChat or one of the other apps on your phone and start texting with your friends. I find texting with new friends who can only speak Mandarin to be the best.

When texting and speaking with others, don't worry about being right, just try to get your idea across. Think about native English speakers you know who speak incorrectly, but you can easily understand what they're talking about. They still probably end up getting their point across.

Continue to ask your teacher how to say new phrases and continue to experiment in the field texting new friends and trying to express new ideas. Do this everyday.

CHAPTER 10

TRANSPORTATION
IN CHINA

MODES OF TRANSPORTATION

GETTING AROUND IN CHINA is relatively easy. Each mode of transportation has its own quirks, but in general it is easy to get around. As with Europe's cities, China's cities are also very efficient and each neighborhood has all the shops and restaurants you are likely to need. Unlike everywhere outside of Manhattan in the United States, you will not need a car for living.

Car

Owning a car is a sign of wealth and prestige in modern day China. Most people want a car and it is usually the first big purchase a person makes. Because of the sheer number of people in China, the roads can become very crowded in cities. I don't recommend buying a car for this reason, though you may want to think about it if you are planning on living in China for a while.

Motorbike

This transportation mode is a favorite among farmers and propane tank and water jug delivery drivers. Keep an eye out for motorbikes carrying two halves of a pig on the back as they are definitely interesting! You can buy a motorbike, but you need a license to drive it legally. Motorbikes are advantageous because they are cheap and don't require much gas. You can also go straight to the front of the lines of traffic waiting at a light, or drive on the sidewalks when necessary in some cities.

Electric Bike

Electric bikes, sometimes resembling motorbikes, sometimes resembling bicycles, are a common mode of transportation and I still don't know why they aren't more common in the United States. Maybe they are illegal. You can buy an electric bike for 700-3,000 RMB and don't need any sort of license. They can go fairly fast, so wear a helmet and be careful. They are also very quiet. This is my transportation mode of choice in China.

Bicycle

Bicycle is still a popular form of transportation. There are a wide variety of bikes available depending where you go. If you want a higher-end bike, you will need to go to a store that caters to bike enthusiasts, rather than people who just want to get from the apartment, to work, to the market, and back. A decent bike can be had for a few hundred RMB. Just make sure you lock it up to something when parking it.

Subways

The subway system in China is very good in most places and is set up the same way as everywhere else in the world. You can get a subway card or buy a ticket each time you want to ride from a machine outside the gates. Most big cities have a subway system and if they don't there is probably one being built currently.

Taxis and Motorbike Taxis

Not only is speaking with taxi drivers one of the best ways to improve your Mandarin quickly, it is also cheap. Most rides around town will cost you between 7 and 20 RMB. When riding in a taxi, it is best to always make sure that drivers use their meter. Sometimes you will see them lining up to wait for passengers exiting a train or bus station. These taxi drivers will sometimes try to get you to pay a flat rate and agree on the price ahead of time. To avoid being ripped off, it is always best to go by the meter.

For a cheaper, yet more dangerous option than a cab, look for a motorbike taxi. If you are walking down the street, hear someone honk, and turn to see a motorbike driver whizzing by watching you, chances are he or she is a motorbike taxi driver. Negotiate with them before you take off.

Buses

The most common mode of transportation is bus. There are buses plying highways from Hong Kong to Beijing as well as convenient city buses around even the smallest cities. Buses that go between cities are generally around 10 RMB for each hour travelled if it is an older bus. For newer buses, it may cost around 40 RMB for one hour of travel time. Each city usually has a main bus station at which you can find buses that go all over the province and country. Such places are usually filled with people from all over China and make for good people watching. Many hotels also serve as small bus stations.

City buses are usually 1-2 RMB per ride and need correct change or a bus card. These buses crisscross the entire city and go to smaller towns and villages as well.

Trains

China is well connected by train. The network of rails goes all over the country, including to Lhasa in Tibet, and if you're planning on going there by train, you can—just make sure you are ready for a 48-hour ride. It is well worth it though as the scenery is amazing.

There are several types of trains in China. Trains designated with a K, T, or Z are older trains that run all over the country. The G and D trains are the sleek, new bullet trains that travel hundreds of kilometers per hour. One can now go from Guangzhou, a big city outside of Hong Kong and the biggest city in Guangdong province, to Beijing in eight hours. Insane, but awesome. It will cost about the same as a one-way plane ticket (800 RMB).

There are generally two types of train stations in China now: high-speed rail stations and normal train stations. High-speed rail stations are usually situated on the edge of the city and the normal train stations, which sometimes accommodate high-speed trains, are located in the center of the city. The older trains are not usually as clean as the newer trains, but they are still fine as long as the people around you are not loud or smoking.

Train tickets are sold two weeks in advance. If you try to buy tickets any earlier than this, you will likely not be able to reserve a ticket yet. I generally buy tickets at the train station in person, but it is now possible to buy tickets online as well.

Planes

Plane travel in China is the same as everywhere else in the developed world. Major airlines include China Eastern, Air China, and Spring Airlines.

CHAPTER 11

FOOD

RESTAURANTS

"DO YOU LIKE RICE or noodles?" one enthusiastic student asked me early on in my teaching career.

I thought about it a moment, having never thought of this question before and answered, "Noodles."

"Me too," the boy said excitedly.

The Chinese culture has a solid eating tradition and part of this tradition relies upon eating a "staple" food of either rice or noodles with every meal. The exception to this is if one is having bread with the meal or dumplings.

One thing you will be doing often in China is ordering food in restaurants. This may be intimidating at first, but with practice and exploration, you will find many Chinese restaurants with food you will like.

Many restaurants will have picture menus. Sometimes there will be pictures of dishes on the walls and you will be able to order by pointing to the picture you find most delicious that day. Other restaurants will have some English written next to each Chinese name in the menu. Oftentimes the translations will be humorous. It's not uncommon to find dishes such as "explode the chicken" or "fragrant fish slivers."

Eating in China is a casual affair. There is no tipping, so don't worry about it. Oftentimes one person will order for the entire table, but when out with friends, it's more common for everyone to order their own dish or for each person to pick a dish and then share.

Usually one person will pay for everyone at the meal with the understanding that the next time you all go out someone else will pay. The exception to this is if you are out with your boss or a superior and in these cases that person will usually pay for the meal. When out with friends, it is common to split the bill. This is sometimes also referred to as "AA" or "Going Dutch" in China.

Eating out in restaurants is done family style. There will be several dishes including meat and vegetables in the middle of the table for everyone to share. Each person will have a bowl filled with rice. During the meal, everyone takes from the center with his or her chopsticks. Sometimes fruit may be served at the end of the meal as dessert.

There are many different types of restaurants with specific types of foods. If I am by myself, I will have several restaurants that I rotate between where I can get a meal for 10-30 RMB. It should be noted that food eaten in restaurants can be the same price as food bought in a grocery store. It's very easy to find food from a small, hole-in-the-wall place that is the same price or cheaper than food found in the supermarket. It's for this reason that eating out in China is very common. I usually eat out twice per day in China.

When ordering in restaurants, you will need to get the waiter or waitress's attention if it is busy. You will not have a specific waiter or waitress and because there are no tips, service can sometimes be spotty. It's for this reason that people will often shout *fuwuyuan* (waiter) or hold their hand up and snap their fingers. This is not considered rude and is just another China quirk.

One of the most useful Chinese phrases to learn is "*Wo yao zhe ge*" which means "I want this one." Use this sentence when ordering. I still use this phrase daily while in China seven years after first arriving.

SUPERMARKET

As was mentioned in Chapter eight, most malls will have a supermarket where you can buy most things you will need to cook and eat.

At first glance, a Chinese supermarket may look the same as in your home country. It sells milk, eggs, bread, peanut butter, Nutella, fruits, vegetables, crackers, chips, soda, etc. They also sell products which cater specifically to a Chinese consumer: frozen dumplings, frozen bean paste buns, dried squid, chili paste, a wide range of mushrooms, and other spices and herbs.

There are also some products which may freak some people out: strange cuts of meat with lots of bones or fat in it, live fish tanks, live frog buckets, live eels, beef candy, and shrimp flavored chips.

Generally, supermarkets are quite clean and will be great places to get everything you need. Three-fourths of the time I needed to buy groceries in China I went to the supermarket. There are also convenience stores and small supermarkets all over the place, which also sell many of the products above. Prices at supermarkets are non-negotiable.

WET MARKET

Wet markets are located all over each city and range from a few people sitting in a back alley selling meat and vegetables to a covered marketplace with more than a hundred stalls selling fruits, vegetables, spices, pork, beef, lamb, chicken, snakes, frogs, crocodiles, and animals you've never seen or heard of. If I am cooking something from scratch and don't need anything extra from the supermarket, I may go to a wet market and buy the fruits and vegetables I need. I'm sure the meat at the wet market is fine, but it's a little too graphic and dirty for me. The prices at the wet market are the cheapest around and you will probably be able to bargain a little.

STREET FOOD

In addition to eating in restaurants, there are also many street-side vendors serving all different kinds of food. This type of food will be some of the cheapest you will find, but the quality can sometimes be questionable.

In the mornings, there may be vendors serving up breakfast foods such as porridge, dumplings, or dim sum (small plates of dumplings and other dishes). This is usually very cheap and you will be able to order quite a lot of food for not much money. For example chicken porridge, a side of vegetables, and a small plate of dumplings might only cost you 10 RMB.

After supper, tables will be set up along sidewalks serving up fried noodles, meat, and vegetables. This is served up with Chinese brews as well as foreign beers such as Pabst Blue Ribbon.

IMPORT STORES

If you can't find something at the supermarket or wet market, you may be able to find it at an import store. Bigger and more developed cities usually have import stores, and a few smaller cities also have import stores, so even if you live in a smaller city, make sure you take a good look around.

Here, for double the price of what you would pay back home you will be able to find spaghetti sauce, sausages, Doritos, many kinds of foreign beer and wine, avocados, canned foods, coffee, and a lot more popular foreign brands. There is a chain of German stores called Metro (*Mai de long*) and they will have everything you are likely to need. Most supermarkets will also have an import aisle, which will have things like spaghetti sauce and noodles, Nutella, and cereal.

FOOD CHARACTERS TO WATCH FOR

Maria was one of the cutest girls I had ever met. She was kind, sweet, feminine, fiery, had an amazing smile, and a great laugh. We were getting along well on our second date and now we were taking a post dinner walk through the back streets of Zhongshan, one of my all time favorite activities.

We rounded a corner passing a Guangdong *diaolou*, an ancient tower employing European architecture, and Maria started to skip ahead of me towards something.

"*Ni qu na?*" Where are you going? I asked her.

She made her way towards a street vendor who had some different foods on display through the glass window of his cart. I looked at the food on display, most of it different types of meat.

"What are you getting?" I asked.

"*Ji zhuazi.*" Chicken feet.

So much for my hopes of a make out, all I could think about was a toenail being stuck between her teeth and me dislodging it by accident and swallowing it later that night.

Interesting Foods

China has a lot of interesting foods, and below is just a short preview. If you see these characters on the menu, you may want to stay away, or try them depending on your mood that day.

■ 鸡爪子 (*ji zhuaji*) Chicken feet.
  The United States exports a lot of these to China.

■ 鸭脖子 (*ya bozi*) Duck neck.
A favorite for something salty to gnaw on.

■ 蟑螂 (*zhang lang*) Cockroach
Yum.

■ 虫 (*chong*) Worm
There are many types, those I have tried are small and fried, having almost no taste and are crunchy.

Chinese Menus

You can learn a lot of Chinese characters by looking at menus and ordering food with little effort. When you are at a restaurant, take a good look at the characters. Don't be intimidated by them. Look for the same character repeated multiple times in each dish's name. You will be surprised by how many you see repeated. This is because each area of the menu is divided into different types of dishes. See below for characters to look for and what each means.

■ 粥 (*zhou*) Porridge
Rice and water usually mixed with some meat or vegetables depending on the dish.

■ 肉 (*rou*) Meat
If the dish has this character in the name, there will be some type of meat present.

■ 饭 (*fan*) Rice
Many dishes end with this and it means white rice is usually served with it or that it is a type of fried rice.

■ 狗 (*gou*) Dog
My Chinese friend tells me they only eat the dumb dogs.

■ 骨 (*gu*) Bone
If this is in the name of the dish, the meat will have bones in it. I try to avoid these dishes.

■ 汤 (*tang*) Soup
This character at the end of a dish's name indicates it's a soup.

■ 面 (*mian*) Noodle
A noodle dish.

■ 肠 (*chang*) Intestines
It is common for dishes to include intestines or other inner organs of animals. This is a good character to learn early on if you don't want to accidentally order something you will not want to eat.

CHAPTER 12

DATING IN CHINA

CROSS CULTURAL ROMANCE

DO CHINESE GIRLS LIKE foreign guys?

I am asked this question a lot by inquisitive friends and acquaintances. The answer is that it depends. Many Chinese girls like foreign guys. On the other hand, there are also many girls that don't want to date foreigners. Those that can speak English and live in bigger cities are more likely to date foreigners.

Do Chinese guys like foreign girls?

I'm not asked this question very often, but the answer is that it also depends. Certainly many Chinese men hold foreign women in high acclaim, but there are also plenty of Chinese guys that don't have any desire to date a foreigner. Again, usually those who can speak some English or have an interest in foreign culture would be open to dating a foreigner.

If you are interested in dating in China, read on for a crash course of what is possible with a little charm and patience.

A TYPICAL FIRST MEETING

A lot of foreigners back home have the image of China as a paradise where Chinese babes are throwing themselves at the feet of even the greasiest of foreigners. This has never happened to anyone I know.

Oftentimes, meeting someone new in China will require that you speak some Mandarin Chinese. Below is a common situation you may find yourself in when meeting a member of the opposite sex. I am writing from the male perspective but many of the principals and sentences spoken here will also apply to women.

Woman: Hello.

Unless you are famous or extremely good looking, you probably don't get a curious "hello" from cute girls in your home country, especially at a mall buying garbage bags in the middle of the day. This is a major advantage when dating in China. The girls will sometimes come to you, and everyone at least knows the word "hello".

If you do need to initiate the conversation (as you usually still will need to do), a simple "hello" or "*nihao*" will do the trick just fine. People usually don't notice the first word you say to them anyway, and it's just a way to break the ice. A friendly grunt may even do the trick if you have lots of confidence.

Nick: *Ni hui shuo yingwen ma?* Can you speak English?

Language is a great conversation topic and I will show you why in a moment. It's also something that is very easy and relevant to talk about. This is why I like to ask this question early on.

Woman: *Wo bu hui.* I can't.

Regardless of whether she can or can't, this is also a good set up for later suggesting that you can help her practice her English. That is unless she brings it up first, which she might.

Woman: *Wode yingwen hen lan.* My English is terrible.

Many Chinese people will tell you that their English is terrible.

Nick: *Wo keyi bang ni lianxi.* I can help you practice.

This assumes you are interested in learning more about her, but you will probably want to wait until further into the conversation to make sure she is the kind of person you want to get to know more.

Woman: *Hao.* Okay.

When arranging a meeting, the goal is to get to know her. Many Chinese girls like to be considered "friends" before being considered to be dating a person anyway.

Nick: *Ni jiao shenme mingzi?* What's your name?

After speaking to someone for this long and you'd like to continue to speak with them, it's generally a good time to ask for their name.

Woman: *Wo jiao Xiao Xue.* My name is Little Snow.

This is a nickname. Chinese names are typically three characters long, the first character being the family name and the last two the given name. When creating nicknames, the character for "little" is often put in front of one character of the given name, in this case "snow." I usually call a person by the name they tell me at this point. Many people will have an English name if they can speak some English.

Nick: *Nide weixin haoma shi shenme?* What's your We-Chat ID?

Little Snow: *Yao ba san* . . . One, eight, three . . .

WHERE TO MEET

This section is devoted to giving you ideas on where to meet potential partners in China.

Friends of Colleagues

Some of the first friends you will make in China will be your colleagues. They will likely have Chinese friends they can introduce to you over dinner. It is perfectly normal to date a friend of a friend and I recommend doing this if possible.

Malls and Shopping Areas

Anywhere that has many people wandering around stopping to browse to see what is on sale is a great place to start. One of my favorite activities is going for a walk and seeing who I meet. Because you are foreigner, you will stick out and usually be able to catch the eye of at least one admirer.

Bars

This is generally a good way to meet a lot of people quickly but the numbers you collect will not likely be the kinds of people you will be able to have a future conversation with, even if your Mandarin is fluent. In my experience with the bar crowd, it's only about ten percent of the numbers I get of people that I end up going on a date with and only a much smaller percentage of these that actually work out.

Online

Just like in many parts of the world, online dating is taking off in China too. Almost every young person's first major purchase of their lives is a smart phone, and online apps are becoming a good way to meet people. Below are some of the options.

■ **Momo** (www.immomo.com/?v=en)
Momo is the most popular dating app in China. It lets one look at pictures and profiles of people in the vicinity

and one is able to send a message to anyone else. I've always had a low response rate, but I've also gone on more than a few dates with people I've met on Momo and some of them turned out to be really interesting people.

■ **Tinder** (www.gotinder.com)
Tinder is an app where people are able to swipe left or right in order to tell a person they like them. If two people both like each other, then they are able to send each other messages. Because the app uses pictures from your Facebook account, you will need a VPN to use it.

■ **Skout** (www.skout.com)
A dating app.

■ **Tantan** (https://tantanapp.com)
Tantan is the most popular dating app in China. It functions the same way as Tinder.

■ **Badoo** (https://badoo.com)
A popular dating app in China.

■ **WeChat** (www.wechat.com/en/)
Instead of asking for a phone number, WeChat may be an even better bet, and I usually opt for this now. WeChat has become one of the most popular phone apps for communicating with friends in China. With over 500 million users as of 2015, it provides a great way to make friends. Besides being the most common means of communication with friends in China, it has a few functions for meeting new people. One of the ways is through the *fujinren* or "nearby people". This function will show you a list of people nearby and you may contact them. I've never met any strangers with WeChat, but it's a good way to stay in touch with friends at least.

■ **Skype** (www.skype.com/en/)
"You better not be a stalker," I joked with the girl I had

just met on Skype. We talked about meeting up sometime and I wanted to gauge her reaction.

"Better be careful," she said after laughing. She had a good sense of humor, and was a lot of fun to banter with.

I have had some fantastic luck with Skype. You should be able to do a search of people in your area and filter by gender and age. Send out a spray of messages and see who replies. Look for profiles of people wanting to practice English. Some people might see this as dishonest, but wait until you meet them in person to decide if you would like to continue to hang out with them or not.

■ **Couch Surfing** (www.couchsurfing.com)

I met a beautiful Russian girl on Couch Surfing who was simply looking for someone to hang out with. She is now a friend. Couch Surfing is an excellent resource for making new friends and you will likely have a lot in common as you are both travelers. Couch Surfing allows a person to display pictures of their home and make it available for anyone traveling through the area who needs a place to stay for free. You can also indicate if your couch is available or not or if you would simply like to meet up for coffee. I've never stayed on anyone's couch or had anyone stay on mine, but I've met several people for coffee, some of whom became friends.

Other Dating Sites

There are a whole slew of sites out there and many will let you check if there are others in your area first before you sign up. Some of these include OK Cupid, Plenty of Fish, Asian Friendfinder, Asian Dating, and Match. I haven't used these in China, but I'm sure at least some of them are a good bet.

THE FIRST DATE

Restaurant
I recommend somewhere you've been before that you know will be good and not too loud so that you can talk. I like to go for sushi and sit at the bar.

Bar
This is probably not the best bet for a first date if you want to get to know the other person.

Mall
Walking around the mall and stopping for coffee or tea is a great option.

Park
Simply going for a walk through the park is good. If you want a little privacy, this is a decent option as most of the other places listed here will have lots of people around.

Bowling
Some cities have bowling alleys and she will likely never have been bowling before since bowling is not very popular or even known in China by most people.

Biking
This is usually a fun activity.

Movies
There are movie theaters all over China. Chinese people love Hollywood movies and there is at least one playing in most cinemas at all times. It will be in English with Chinese subtitles.

I recommend combining two of the above options. My usual first date is going to dinner and then going for a short walk either in a park or down a street lined with shops.

On the first date, try to do most of the talking yourself. Express your feelings and reactions to events in your life so that you don't come across as closed and they can be comfortable with you. Obviously also make sure you are listening and not just talking the entire time. This will prompt her to talk about her own life and her feelings and reactions towards it.

Some girls may talk about already having a boyfriend. Some girls will tell you they don't want to date right now. Don't fall for this trap. A person's true thoughts, feelings, and priorities are represented by their actions, not by their words. If they are on a date with you there is a good chance they are interested in you. I believe guys are more obvious with how they feel, but it can be difficult for a guy to know what a woman is thinking or feeling if he goes purely by what she is saying. This is probably true of women not knowing what men are thinking as well.

I once met a girl who seemed like a total jerk at our first meeting, saying nasty things about foreigners. At first, the conversation was rough, but by being patient and not judging, I was able to get her to let her guard down and open up. We ended up dating.

Usually a person will say negative things because they are scared. In the above girl's case, I believe she had met some foreigners who were jerks to her or people she knew. A girl may tell you she has a boyfriend if she doesn't want to hang out with you or doesn't see boyfriend potential in you.

When speaking English, don't use colloquialisms or uncommon words. Pay attention to this or she won't understand what you are saying if her English isn't great. It's usually a good idea to have a pen and small notebook nearby as learning each other's language is a great topic and a great chance for both of you to learn more of the other's language.

BUILDING RAPPORT

Going on a second date and then future dates is obviously the next step towards building a relationship. The key towards getting second and third dates often lies in texting. This is also where massive language learning takes place, so read on.

As we have already discussed, the best way to get better at Mandarin, or any language, is to use it. We have seen how you can use it when speaking with others in public. However as you will likely already know, when first starting to use a new language it can be extremely difficult to understand what a person is saying and come up with responses on the fly like you can in your native language. It is for this reason that texting, or any form of writing back and forth with a time buffer, is so valuable.

In order to illustrate the advantages of learning Mandarin via text message, I have created a dialogue between a Chinese woman with the English name of Marie and myself, and include commentary on the process as we go along.

I'm walking back to my apartment from my 4:00 p.m. class and decide to send Marie, a woman I met at the supermarket a week ago, who I went on a date with the previous night, a message via WeChat.

Nick: *Ni chi fan le ma*? Have you eaten yet?

This is a common phrase in China, and it is actually more akin to asking someone, "How are you?" as a way of showing concern for their well being. If you can't think of anything else to start with, this is a fine phrase to use.

You will probably want to type in *pinyin* when first starting to learn Mandarin and the other person will likely understand what you are saying since most people in China understand *pinyin*. Otherwise, most phones now have built in ways of typing characters, which typically rely on typing the *pinyin* and selecting the character you would like. The most frequent characters and phrases pop up first.

Marie: *Wo chi le. Ni ne?* I ate already. What about you?

Nick: *Wo ye chi le. Ni jintian zuo le shenme?* I ate too already. What did you do today?

If you do not know how to formulate a response in real time, texting allows you the time to formulate one. If you do not know how to say what you'd like to, take the time to look up the word or words in a dictionary, or consult your learning materials if they are at hand. You will improve dramatically if you do this and continue to push yourself to make up new phrases to text your new friends.

Marie: *Wo zai gongsi shangban le.* I was working at my company all day.

"*Gongsi*" and "*shangban*" are both very common words and will likely come up in some of your first conversations. They mean "company" and "working" respectively.

Nick: *Nide gongzuo zai nali.* Where is your company?

In this situation "*gongzuo*" means "work" and is roughly the same as "job" or "company." The above grammatical construction is also very common when asking where something is located. "*Zai*" means "at" in this context. Therefore the sentence literally reads "Your company at where?".

KNOWING WHEN TO STOP PURSUING

As I've mentioned before, one of the most important things to learn in dating is when to call it quits. You're gaga for a girl. She's fiery, sexy, flirtatious, smart, and witty. You really want it to work out between the two of you, but you just can't get her to come out on a third date. She responds to all your text with one or two word answers. Anytime you try to ask her out she deflects with "I'm busy," "I don't feel well," or "I'm tired." If more than three of these indicators are received in a row, it's probably time to erase them from your phone. If they are indeed interested, the time you give them could be the thing they need for the relationship to be reignited, but otherwise suck it up and move on.

In China, it can be particularly difficult to tell what a girl really thinks of you. She may refer to you as her "older (or younger) brother" an affectionate name for a man she considers a friend. You might think that this means you are no longer a contender, but in actuality she may very well still like you, so don't worry if she calls you this.

DATING OTHER FOREIGNERS

Before closing, I would also like to mention that while in China, dating other foreigners is much easier than in one's home country (at least this is true for guys in the United States). Men and women seem to be attracted to each other more in China than they are in their home country. I am not sure why, maybe because they are more rare. As a guy in the United States a girl may not give you a second glance, but because you might be the first foreigner she's seen in a week in China, she will likely do a double take. I know I usually do whenever I see another foreigner in a small city in China.

Take advantage of this scarcity effect. You will be able to strike up conversations with the opposite sex much more easily than in your home country as you will have much more to talk about and they will likely welcome speaking with another foreigner.

CHAPTER 13

A NIGHT IN ZHONGSHAN

NIGHTLY ACTIVITIES IN CHINA

WALKING ALONG THE PALM-LINED street in Zhongshan are the nightly passersby. They are the typical crowd: factory workers, students, families, senior citizens, and the occasional foreigner from a nearby swanky hotel, in town on business out exploring the city.

My brother also teaches English in China and after supper with some students we are sitting at an outdoor café watching the crowds. The heat of the day has dissipated and it is now in the twenties (Celsius), cool enough for an evening stroll. The café offers a variety of teas, snacks, and beer. I'm partial to Jasmine milk tea and my brother likes *tie guan yin*, a green tea.

An older couple walks by in their pajamas, two students smile in surprise as they spot us in the café. Out of the crowd walks our friend, Dean. He's driven all the way from Shenzhen, a nearby city, bigger than New York City, across the border from Hong Kong and an hour's drive from Zhongshan. "Are you guys ready for a crazy night?" he asks us.

Massages

We have just finished eating and so the three of us make our way to a nearby massage parlor. We are led upstairs and into a room with several comfortable armchairs and a TV. We are asked some questions about what types of tea or coffee we'd like to drink as well as the type of massage we would like.

After a moment, a server returns with our drinks and plates of complimentary fruit. Soon after, three masseuses come in with hot buckets of water for our feet to be dipped in prior to the foot massage. We relax and enjoy the conversation and massages.

Besides being a great place to relax, making conversation with the masseuses is also one of the best ways to practice Mandarin as a beginner. They will ask you typical questions that any new person you meet in China will ask you, such as where you are from and how old you are. The foot massage lasts about an hour and costs 40 RMB.

Massage parlors are all over China and you can find many different types including foot massage, body massage, body massage with oil, Thai massage, and some type of massage where they walk on your back. These types of massages are a little more expensive and may cost around 100 RMB at some places.

Chinese Clubs and Bars

After our massages, we make our way towards a city center. Here, next to one of the rivers that cut through the city, there are a plethora of clubs and bars catering to both foreigners and Chinese alike. Preferring the Chinese clubs with their loud music, extravagant layouts, and attractive waitresses, we take a look at several to see which is the most happening that night. Even in small cities in China like Zhongshan there are numerous clubs and bars.

We head into Miumiu, a bar next to the newly built Sheraton Hotel. Inside we're greeted by the posse of young hipsters that are every club's staff. Inside the club it's like we've entered the Foot Clan's lair from Ninja Turtles. It looks like a parking garage, but with neon green and orange lights, lots of tables, and a stage for the DJ, a performer, and dancing.

Lulu, a Chinese girl with giant heels, long black hair, and fake eyelashes comes over to take our order by yelling into my ear from two inches away. I yell back that we'll take a bottle of whiskey. One must order either a bucket of beers or a bottle of alcohol at a club in China. If you order a single drink, it will cost as much as it does at a club in the United States or Europe, sometimes more.

To get a table in a Chinese club you will need to pay a minimum amount of money. You cannot order just a few drinks. The minimum is usually around 200-300 RMB but I've also been to places where it's around 700 RMB.

Our alcohol appears along with serving boys who mix the green tea and Johnnie Walker Red Label together in a pitcher and then pour it into our glasses. Green tea or red tea usually comes with whiskey to be mixed in. This is a very popular club drink in China and is smooth. Our waitress hangs around with us drinking our whiskey for a few minutes in order to build some rapport as our host so that we will come back to the club next time. Hosts like this also spend a lot of time texting previous clientele to come to the bar that night. Lulu notices a few foreign faces in the club and leaves the three of us to enjoy the atmosphere, which we do well. We continue to drink and chat with other groups around the club, collecting lots of phone numbers of people we probably won't call.

Around 2 a.m., as the height of the party is subsiding a little, we head outside where we can hear each other more easily. From here we have two options: we can check out a karaoke place, order food, and sing some songs, or we can check out a nearby bar.

There are two kinds of bars in China: foreigner bars and Chinese bars. The foreigner bars are similar to bars in the United States and Europe. The Chinese bars try to emulate the foreigner bars, but the atmosphere is usually a little quieter. At the foreigner bars you will be able to find some foreign beers on tap. It will of course cost a lot more too. Foreign brews typically can't be found at the Chinese bars. If we do go out, my friends and I typically just go to a Chinese club since it's a lot more fun than a foreigner or Chinese bar. Therefore, we decide to go with the next option.

Karaoke
The glitzy hallways of the Karaoke establishment look like the interior of a space ship, and singing comes from every direction. We get a small room big enough for a small group of friends, order some beer, and choose our favorite songs.

This is the perfect opportunity to show off Chinese singing skills, unfortunately there is no one around to impress but each other. Still, belting out some Beyond and Chopstick Brothers, two high-quality Chinese bands, is very satisfying.

Karaoke in China is done in rooms made for five to ten people typically, though there are rooms fit for thirty or more people. In China, it's common for friends to go out at night singing karaoke. If you teach English in China, you will probably wind up here with your students as well at some point. There are songs in both Mandarin and English usually, as well as Cantonese, Japanese, and Korean. Your students will love it if you sing some English songs with them at karaoke.

Late Night Dinner

Around 4 a.m., we decide to get something more substantial to eat than the free peanuts and watermelon offered at karaoke. We take a cab to get some *da pai dang* or *xiao ye*: late night dinner. The street side vendors and restaurants that are often set up on the side of the street or in a space that's typically a parking lot or wet market by day, are restaurants servicing some delicious fare by night. Like most businesses in China, as long as there are customers, they stay open.

We find a place on the edge of the city in a neighborhood that none of us has been to before. At the center of the maze of old streets and architecture is a giant square filled with hungry and tipsy Chinese.

We find a table near the edge of the hubbub and order our dishes: fried noodles, lamb kebabs, barbecued chicken, shrimp and crab porridge, and green vegetables with garlic.

These types of restaurants vary in their variety and quality. There are usually places on the side of the road serving up fried noodles and dumplings, but these can sometimes be a little too greasy. The places where you will find much better food are often restaurants by day and then they will set out tables at night on the sidewalk. Or there will be a big area filled with tables where people are eating porridge or some other special and delicious dishes. If you don't know of any such places ask a cab driver or any bar goer, as they will definitely know a good place.

At this point, we are all somewhere between buzzed and drunk. The random yelling and drunken slurs are subsiding around us. We look at the surrounding destruction: bottles, tissues, and chicken bones scattered on the floor. I look at my phone and see it is after six. Looking up, I notice that the sky is definitely lighter. There is a long line of cabs waiting nearby and we take one back to our apartments.

Another great night in Zhongshan.

CHAPTER 14

TRAVEL IN CHINA

OFF THE BEATEN PATH TRAVEL

THERE ARE MANY RESOURCES out there for many of the typical travel destinations. If you are looking for this information I would recommend checking out the CNN Travel website or the next section of this guide.

However, many of the places that are popular in China have huge crowds, and if you are like me, after a while, such crowded attractions, which can also be very expensive, begin to lose the natural beauty and mystery they once possessed. That is why I go on Google Earth and grill my friends, figuring out interesting places around China that not a lot of tourists go to. The following is a brief list of such places.

The time of year you travel could also affect your experience. Some villages may be very crowded during the Chinese holidays or on weekends, but empty at other times. Use this knowledge to your advantage. For information on how to get to each of these places, click on the links next to each place's name. They link to my website, China

Life Files, where I have written more in depth information about each place.

■ **Wenhai and Tiger Leaping Gorge** (www.chinalife-files.com/travel/wenhai-yunnan/)

The valleys surrounding Jade Dragon Snow Mountain in northwestern Yunnan province contain picturesque paths through mountains and villages untainted by tourism. My travel companions and I were surprised by the lack of people on our hike along the foot of the mountain as we made our way from Lijiang, a famous travel destination known for its wooden houses and streams running through the city, to Wenhai, a tiny village unknown to most tourists on the other side of one of the great mountain legs thrown out by Jade Dragon Snow Mountain.

Wenhai itself looked deserted at first glance, as no one was outside this tiny farming community. However, over the course of our two-night stay at the Wenhai Eco Lodge, which was mostly spent relaxing and strolling through the nearby forests, we did meet some locals. They spoke Mandarin with a heavy accent so it was difficult to have much conversation.

From Wenhai, we rode horses for four hours through a gorge and out onto a main road. From here, we took a van with a driver that we found at a roadside eatery along the Yangtze River. The next leg of our journey would be hiking and staying at inns along the Tiger Leaping Gorge, a gorge made by the Yangtze River cutting between Jade Dragon Snow Mountain and Haba Snow Mountain, several miles to the north.

Our two-night stay along the trail was filled with food from the mountains, hot showers, and warm beds. The scenery was beautiful and it was perfect hiking weather for February at around ten degrees Celsius during the day. These were a magical five days and I hope you get a chance to do the same thing.

■ **Huzhu Beishan and Heaven Lake** (www.chinalife-files.com/travel/huzhu-beishan-heaven-lake-qinghai/)

Before moving back home to the United States for the first time after living in China, I wanted to visit my friend, Tommy, in Qinghai province, where he was from.

We first saw the normal sites of Xining city and the surrounding area, which included the rolling hills of the Tibetan Plateau, Tibetan monasteries, Qinghai Lake (China's largest lake), and ate enough lamb to satisfy even me—my favorite Chinese food. It was now time to find somewhere off the beaten path.

In the mountains along the border of Qinghai and Gansu provinces, to the north of Xining city, is Heaven Lake. Tommy is also an avid adventurer and now runs his own adventure travel business. He knew of a place up in the mountains that not a lot of people would go, even during the peak travel season (it was now July). Thus, we made our way to Huzhu Beishan Park, where we would find the trail leading to the lake.

After walking through the park for a few hours, we met a Tibetan man who told us the way to Heaven Lake. The man offered to give us a ride by motorbike to the foot of the trail, but since we needed to rest for the evening before making the journey, we didn't take him up on his offer.

The next morning, after staying at a guesthouse that night with a Tibetan host family, we did make it up into the mountains. Along the way, we passed a few tiny houses perched precariously on the cliff side. The people here were shepherds and their goats dotted the hillsides.

It was misty up in the mountains and it wasn't so obvious where the lake would be. Fortunately, a family allowed us to have lunch with them in one of their small houses along the mountain path. The husband agreed to show us the way up the mountain, although it was his wife who told us this as the man had lost his tongue at a young age, so could not speak clearly.

The old man did lead us through the mist to the lake at the top of the mountain. The scenery and lake were beautiful, and the kindness of the Tibetan people made the trip that much better.

◼ Sai Wan and Tai Long Wan (www.chinalifefiles. com/2013/09/09/sai-wan-hong-kong/)

Hong Kong is one of the most densely packed cities in the world. Its name often conjures up a sub tropical, Asian New York City—a maze of concrete and palm trees. Nevertheless, the former British colony actually has more green space than city, and my fellow colleagues and I were about to experience this first hand.

We had taken a subway, three buses, and were now walking along the Luk Wo Country Trail in Sai Kung Park. Our destination was purportedly the most beautiful beach in Hong Kong: Tai Long Wan. As it was hours away from the central city of Hong Kong, and a weekday, we hoped we'd have the three-kilometer stretch of sand and green hills to ourselves.

It took us an hour and a half to hike all the way to the beach, but it was well worth it. Besides one or two small groups of people we had the entire place to ourselves. It being August, the water was like bath water. We lazed about the rest of the afternoon and got a nice sunburn.

◼ Huihang Caravan Trail (www. chinalifefiles.com/2013/09/01/ hui-hang-caravan-trail-anhui-province/)

"*Wushi kuai qian yi ge, zui pianyi de,*" the old woman told my brother, trying to get the most money she could for the pecans she was trying to sell him. We'd run into two old ladies during our hike along the Anhui-Hangzhou Caravan Trail, a trail that ran through the mountains between Anhui and Zhejiang provinces and was used for trade hundreds of years ago. The old women were pedaling nuts and they had already come down from their original price of 100 RMB ($15) per bag, and were now offering them for 50 RMB thanks to a little haggling. In China, it's common to haggle for almost everything.

"*Wushi kuai yi ge, wushi kuai, zui pianyide,*" they repeated. 50 RMB was the cheapest price and that is what they'd sell it for. My brother relented, as it was a pretty hefty bag of pecans after all, the kind that would cost you $20 at a super market in the United States.

My brother handed her the money and took the nuts. The old ladies turned to our friend and looked up at him.

"*Ershiwu kuai yi ge, zui pianyide,*" they told him. 25 RMB was now the cheapest price for one bag. We all enjoyed the humor of the situation. There were no laws for how business was to be conducted in these parts of China.

■ **Mogan Mountain** (www.chinalifefiles. com/2012/08/26/renting-a-car-in-china/)
My friend Bill and I had met through a mutual friend shortly after I'd moved to Jiaxing. The road trip we took that first summer was the first of several around Zhejiang province. It was the first time either of us had rented a car in China and we wanted to see what could be seen in a day. One close site that we had heard about was Mogan Shan.

Mogan Shan was a mountain of bamboo forests on the northern edge of Hangzhou city, the capital of Zhejiang province. Our first stop was a restaurant at the top of the mountain which looked out onto the villages tucked into the valleys far below.

After our meal, we walked through the bamboo along a trail winding down the mountain. We passed by several old stone houses. It was likely that none of them were inhabited anymore now that the site was a tourist attraction, but I liked to think that maybe some people still lived in these rustic buildings. We'd heard that there were some mountain biking trails around, but did not see any. We would have to come back again for that. As it was getting late in the day and we still had a two-hour drive left in front of us, we headed back to the parking lot.

POPULAR TRAVEL DESTINATIONS

When people think of traveling in China, several places come to mind. They are usually the most popular places. In my experience traveling throughout the Americas, Europe, and Asia, I've found that it's the off the beaten path places that are more interesting and exciting. A good rule of thumb is that if a place is in a mainstream guidebook like Lonely Planet, there is a fifty percent chance there will be hordes of tourists there.

However, I thought that you will likely be going to some of the more popular spots, so below I've listed some things that are worth seeing at each place as well as my own biased, but very legitimate views.

BEIJING

The Great Wall

When people who have never been to China think of China, they usually think of the Great Wall. The Great Wall is quite epic and should not be missed. The wall winding through the hills may conjure up memories of landscapes from Dr. Seuss books.

There are many areas of the Great Wall to visit and of course the further you are from civilization, the better your time will likely be. If you have time, I recommend renting a car and following the wall west for several hours until you get somewhere with fewer people. I have seen the Great Wall three times in three places, and by far the best portion is from *Simatai* to *Jinshanling*.

This part of the Wall is three to four hours from Beijing, and worth the ride. There are no crowds and you will be free to explore the wall unfettered. Be prepared for a lot of walking and be safe. Many parts of the wall have fallen apart here.

Forbidden City

This is on everyone's list of places to see and I will keep this section brief. After a while most tourist attractions, temples, shrines, etc. look the same. I recommend choosing two or three per week and keeping it at that, otherwise they will begin to blur together. It costs money to get in and closes early in the afternoon around three or four. The Forbidden City consists mainly of a maze of reconstructed rooms and pavilions for you to explore.

Temple of Heaven

The Temple of Heaven is located in a park with many other sights. If you don't want to wait in line at the Forbidden City or deal with lots of tourists, this is a good option.

Summer Palace

Between this and the above two main sites located in Beijing city, this is probably the best. It's a giant palace located on a lake at the northwestern edge of Beijing. This attraction feels less "touristy" than the others do as well.

In general to get a more authentic travel experience I recommend going places where other people are not going. Taking a bus to a city that's not in any guidebook or that Lonely Planet tells you has nothing to see is a good bet. These are the best cities because there's no hype, nobody is trying to sell you anything, and there's no pressure to have a great experience. Try exploring restaurants, bars, and shops for more authentic experiences as well.

SHANGHAI

Shanghai is great. As far as cities go, you will have a hard time finding somewhere more vibrant than Shanghai in China. As for what to see, the best places for eating and drinking, as well as exploring, are Tian Zi Fang and Xin Tian Di.

Tian Zi Fang is a maze of alleyways with shops, restaurants, and bars popular with tourists and locals alike. It's near the Da Pu Qiao subway stop on line 9.

Xin Tian Di consists of a few lanes containing ritzy clubs and restaurants. I once paid over 700 RMB for breakfast at a Taiwanese dim sum restaurant. Come here to see everyone dressed his or her best and trying to have a great time.

After Xin Tian Di and Tian Zi Fang, a great area to check out is the French Concession. There are many old buildings here, with good restaurants, bars, and hotels. This is where I typically stay in Shanghai.

As for tourist sites, there are also some good places. Yu Gardens (*yu yuan*) and the surrounding area are cool if you would like to see Chinese gardens and lots of shops, teahouses, and restaurants selling souvenirs in a cool ambiance.

Nanjing road and The Bund are also worth walking down for their respective neon signs and colonial buildings.

If you'd like to get tailor-made clothing, I recommend checking out the large covered market near Nan Pu Da Qiao subway stop on line 4. An entire floor is devoted to tailored clothing.

XI'AN

The Terra Cotta Soldiers cost at least 350 RMB to see and are quite touristy. If you absolutely must go, then I say go check it out. I have not spent much time around Xi'an but I have read that the surrounding areas of the province are beautiful. There is also a lot of history in the area since this was the original capital of China.

GUILIN

If you like dramatic landscapes and discovering your own gems, this is the best place to check out of the popular destinations.

The dramatic karst landscapes jutting out of Guilin and the surrounding area are why tourists come. It isn't the cities of Guilin and Yangshuo that are interesting, though seeing mountains in the middle of a city is cool, but more the tiny villages and farms you will find biking through the countryside. My advice is to make for Guilin or Yangshuo, rent a bike or motorbike, and explore the countryside on your own.

There are many trails in the area and even during China's busiest travel holiday (the first week in October), you will be able to find a path all to yourself within several kilometers of these city centers.

In addition to exploring the countryside, you may also want to do some rock climbing. This area is world famous for its rock climbing and people come here from all over the world to do it. You can find companies that will take you rock climbing for the day in both Yangshuo and Guilin in the parts of town with lots of hostels.

MACAU

If you had to choose between only seeing Hong Kong or Macau, you would definitely want to choose Hong Kong. In fact, wherever you plan to go in China, Macau should probably be the last place on your list unless you really like gambling, in which case maybe it should be the first.

Macau is home to many casinos and hotels but still pales in comparison to Las Vegas. There are some cool streets with Cantonese and Portuguese architecture, and part of *India Jones and the Temple of Doom* was filmed on one of them. There are some decent areas to check out on the southern island of Taipa as well including Taipa village, which is a maze of old streets with restaurants and old architecture, and Fernando's, a Portuguese restaurant along Hac Sa beach, a black sand beach.

Other than that, I'd say save your days for somewhere like Hong Kong or Zhuhai, the Chinese city just on the other side of Macau and also one of China's cleanest and greenest cities.

HONG KONG

I mention Hong Kong in other parts of this guide, but here I will elaborate in more detail. With its jam-packed streets of neon and dingy back alleys, combined with the lush green hills and islands surrounding Hong Kong, it is the perfect place when you want to get away from the chaos of mainland China.

As a traveler, you will want to check out the surrounding forests, hills, beaches, and islands. Fortunately there are excellent trails and many guides written about this so I will not write further. Some of my favorite trails and beaches are Tai Long Wan (see Off The Beaten Path Travel), Dragon's Back near Shek O, and Tai Tam reservoir just north of Stanley. The trails in each of these places guarantee some beautiful views of Hong Kong and the surrounding hills and islands as well as some great hiking through forest.

Besides hiking and checking out secluded beaches, the city itself has lots to offer. I will extrapolate on the activities available by area.

Central

Central could be considered the main downtown of Hong Kong and besides being home to many giant neon advertisements and banks, it's also got a ton of great bars, restaurants, and shopping opportunities.

The area of Lan Kuai Fong just to the south of Central station is home to the biggest bar scene in Hong Kong.

There are all sorts of places and you will definitely find somewhere you like if you enjoy "clubbing". If you are strapped for cash, there are Seven Elevens all over the city and you can hang out outside of one drinking cheap brews and "pre-gaming" as it's called in some circles, in the sultry Hong Kong heat.

There are also plenty of restaurants in this area, some of which are open twenty-four hours. My favorites to come at any time of day or night include Ebeneezer's, which serves gyros, and Flying Pan, which serves American or British breakfast.

For upscale shopping in this area, go to IFC tower mall or Pacific Place. For cheaper buys, there are some markets every kilometer or so, so just wander and ask. Most people speak English.

The most popular site in the area is Victoria Peak, the highest peak on Hong Kong Island. You can take a tram, or bus if you have time to spare, to the top of the peak and take in some nice views.

It should also be noted that most of Hong Kong's buses are double decker and the views the second floor affords are awesome on some of the bus lines.

Wan Chai

Wan Chai is the old red light district of Hong Kong. There are lots of good bars and restaurants in the area so be sure to take a look. On Sundays during the day many of the bars are packed with Philippine women from noon onwards so be sure to check that out if you are a guy looking for some romance. Wan Chai on any night of the week during the middle of the night is a scene to behold. The party doesn't stop until the morning.

Stanley

To the southeast of Hong Kong Island is the little town

of Stanley. With water surrounding it on almost four sides and green hills rising up behind the town, it is a very quaint place. Some of the most expensive real estate in the world is here and a monthly rent of tens of thousands of US dollars is normal for a two or three bedroom apartment.

Stanley Market sells all kinds of stuff from toys to clothing and souvenirs. It's a nice place to explore when combined with some of the restaurants and bars along the waterfront. There are also some great hiking opportunities in the area, including Dragon's Back and Tai Tam Reservoir. There are some swimming beaches in the area as well, which are generally not too crowded on weekdays.

Tsim Sha Tsui

The southern tip of Kowloon is called Tsim Sha Tsui. Kowloon might be considered the more Chinese part of Hong Kong. It has many small shops and restaurants to check out. Knutsford Terrace has some nice restaurants and bars, similar to those that might be found in Lan Kuai Fong.

Kowloon Park is a beautiful stretch of greenery in the middle of Kowloon. To the east of here is the Hong Kong Museum of History, which is worth a visit. Hong Kong has a very interesting history and is enjoyable to learn about.

Tsim Sha Tsui is also home to Chungking Mansions, a dingy group of buildings with some crusty, yet cheap accommodation. I have never stayed here but some friends have and though it's cheap, they've told me it hasn't been worth it.

The Mansions' saving grace however is an Indian restaurant called Taj Mahal. Go inside and ask around and you will find it on one of the floors. Great food and atmosphere.

Mong Kok

Four subway stops to the north of Tsim Sha Tsui is Mong Kok. This area was once the most densely populated on earth, and it still feels that way. There are hundreds of shops and restaurants to be found among the neon lights and street markets.

The night markets sell lots of touristy things, as well as other items such as photography equipment and knives. Hong Kong is actually one of the best places for photographers to shop. I recommend checking out Wing Shing Photo or Tin Cheung Camera. Some of these stores have branches in Tsim Sha Tsui, another popular camera area.

Sai Kung

Sai Kung is a hilly area to the northwest of central Hong Kong. Here you will find many opportunities for hiking, biking, camping, and eating seafood. The beaches of Tai Long Wan and Sai Long Wan are definitely worth checking out, though it will be a haul coming from central Hong Kong, and it may take three to four hours to get to the beach if you are using public transportation.

Lantau Island

Lantau Island is actually the biggest island in the Hong Kong territory. The airport is located here and so is Hong Kong's Disney Land. It's also home to the Big Buddha statue and Hong Kong's highest peak, Lantau Peak. I recommend taking the gondola up to Big Buddha and checking it out. It's a bit touristy, but it's not often you see a giant Buddha statue on a hill. There are trails nearby leading up to Lantau peak and one can make it to the top but it's a steep climb.

My favorite attraction of Lantau Island is Tai O, a small village on the western tip of the island. It's a sleepy little place with decent seafood and some shops, but the best part is wandering the alleys and enjoying a new place far away from the commotion of the city.

Lamma Island

Lamma Island has some popular beaches, and it is also popular for its seafood. There are some trails to hike, but the trails I did are well worn by other travelers. There may be more trails going off into the hills, but I'm not sure. If interested, it's best get a hiking book or do some research on a website like this one: www.hkoutdoors.com.

ADVENTURE TRAVEL

Rock Climbing

There are places to rock climb all over China. Guilin and Yangshuo in Guangxi province are a mecca for rock climbers in China and it is famous worldwide. Rock climbing here is the same as in many parts of the world. There are many routes that have already been bolted and plenty of outfitters in the surrounding towns to take you to such places. In Chinese, mountain climbing is known as *pan yan* or literally "climb rock."

Doing a Google search will turn up many places to rock climb in China.

Hiking

There are many places to go hiking in China, but the style of hiking differs from place to place. *Pashan* means "climb mountain" but typically refers more to walking up a local hill for exercise on a paved road or path.

Tubu, meaning something like "walk on foot" on the other hand, better matches the idea of hiking in an area far from civilization on a dirt or gravel path. There are many places to do this, but it is usually done by fewer people and can often be harder to find. A good starting point is to go to a popular mountain and look for smaller trails heading off into the wild.

In the Off the Beaten Path Travel section, I introduced

some off the beaten path travel destinations and nearly all have ample hiking opportunities.

Kayaking
Not nearly as well known as rock climbing or hiking, kayaking is new to the adventure travel scene in China.

Coastlines Kayaking (www.coastlineskayak.com/en/index.php) in Fuyang, a city a few hours drive south of Hangzhou, was established around 2010 after the founder fell in love with kayaking on a trip to New Zealand.

At Coastlines, one can rent a kayak for the day and either paddle around the island in the Qian Tang River or go on a longer expedition. Longer expeditions are held at different times throughout the year. Prices are reasonable and lodging is also provided for a fee.

Skiing and Snowboarding
Skiing and Snowboarding are gaining popularity in China, but there is really only one area of China to do it in: Beijing and Dongbei.

Dongbei means northeast and it is the area of China to the northeast of Beijing consisting of Heilongjiang, Jillin, and Liaoning provinces. There are numerous places for skiing in this area of China, as well as in Beijing and surrounding Hebei province.

Outdoor Equipment Stores
A popular chain of outdoor equipment stores in China is Decathlon (*dikanong*). Carrying everything from sleeping bags, tents, and mountain bikes to yoga mats and fishing tackle, Decathlon has a good selection of gear.

Bigger cities that are filled with more people with an interest in adventure sports will find more stores of this nature. Chengdu, the capital of Sichuan province and the largest city in western China has loads of such stores. The city is the gateway to plenty of adventure travel with the Tibetan Plateau just beyond the mountains Sichuan province is famous for. At these stores you can find pots and pans, rock climbing gear, and plenty of clothing.

TRAVEL RESOURCES

■ **Cheap Tickets** (www.cheaptickets.com)
A website for booking plane tickets. Buy several months in advance to get the best deals.

■ **Ctrip** (www.english.ctrip.com)
An excellent Chinese website for booking flights and accommodation. It is primarily for Chinese cities, but also has international flights. I now only use this website for booking accommodation within China.

■ **Hostel World** (www.hostelworld.com)
A website for finding and booking hotels and hostels all over the world.

■ **Agoda** (www.agoda.com)
A site that is virtually the same as Hostel World.

■ **Couch Surfing** (www.couchsurfing.com)
Find strangers in other cities to stay with for free. This can be a good way to meet locals but can be a pain if you're moving every few days and always need to liaise with another person, especially if you're having trouble finding someone, which is common. I like to use it to meet up for coffee or tea with new and interesting people in my own city.

■ **Virtual Tourist** (www.virtualtourist.com)
Virtual Tourist is a social media site where users generate profiles of places to visit, give reviews, and answer questions.

■ **Trippy** (www.trippy.com)
Trippy is a social media site dedicated to asking others unique travel questions about places. While good for asking questions about common travel destinations, you may have difficulty finding people who have been to places other than the popular travel destinations.

■ **CNN Travel** (www.travel.cnn.com/china)
One of the best sites for researching all types of places, popular and unpopular.

■ **Far West China** (www.farwestchina.com/blog)
A website dedicated to travel and living in Xinjiang, China's westernmost province. Xinjiang is also the furthest place from any ocean in the world.

■ **The Land of Snows** (www.thelandofsnows.com)
A website dedicated to travel and living in Tibet. Permits are required for foreigners traveling to Tibet and parts of the province will often be closed to foreigners without notice. Check this website for the most recent updates. The Tibetan plateau also includes most of Sichuan and Qinghai provinces, and this website also has information on these areas.

■ **Lonely Planet Thorn Tree Forum** (www.lonelyplanet.com/thorntree)
Forums where travelers may exchange ideas about world travel. It can have some good information about different trips people have taken.

CHAPTER 15

DEALING WITH CULTURE SHOCK

MAKE A NICE HOME

IF YOU ARE LIKE most foreigners in China, you will inevitably experience culture shock and sometimes homesickness. Maybe a certain person will annoy you, maybe you will grow weary of disorganization of some sort, or maybe you will just miss your friends and family back home. In this section, I give you some ways of dealing culture shock and how to combat it effectively.

One of the best ways of combating culture shock is to make your apartment a place you look forward to going home to. Most places I have lived in China have generally been in a good location with nice amenities as far as Chinese apartments go. Decorate the interior of your apartment with things that remind you of home or make you comfortable. At the same time you do not want to be overly reliant on these little comforts because if you are, you may not ever adapt and integrate into the Chinese culture.

Some things I recommend are warm lighting, a DVD player, a nice rug, some art to hang on the walls, and pictures of family and friends. Other conveniences that may also help include a George Foreman grill, XBOX or other gaming system, and musical instruments if you are musically inclined. Also, spend extra money on some foods that are a little more expensive in China that may remind you of home, such as different cereals. You will be able to buy most of the above in China at shopping malls, music stores, or shops selling artwork.

BE PATIENT AND GO WITH THE FLOW

One skill all successful expats living in China develop is their ability to be patient and go with the flow. You will experience moments when you want things to be like they are back home. Maybe a class is cancelled with no prior notice and you show up to no students in class. Maybe you make plans to go exploring in the mountains of Sichuan, but when you get to the bus station you are told no foreigners are allowed to leave the city for certain areas of the province during the holiday. Or maybe someone remarks that you are fat for the third time in a single day—the Chinese views about being overweight are very different than in some countries and it's not taboo to say someone is fat.

Yes, you may be justified in getting angry and judging the ways things are as feeble. And you may be right. It's okay to get a bit angry and worked up, and don't pretend like something uncomfortable didn't happen if it did. But one of your best allies will be being patient and waiting. Learn to avoid situations that cause too much discomfort.

When in China, I try to never go to the supermarket or shopping mall on weekends because there are too many people and it gets loud and crowded. If I know a particular restaurant is notorious for making different food from what I order, I stay away from it. If one of my colleagues is a jerk, I stay away from him or her.

From time to time, you may also need to follow a system

that seems backward in order to get what you want. Train tickets are only sold a couple weeks before the departure date and so this may make planning trips ahead of time difficult or nerve racking at times. Your school might not tell you your class schedule until the day before classes. You will wonder why you get paid in cash and why the school doesn't just deposit money directly into your account. Whatever the seemingly strange and inefficient system is, don't get worked up about it, go with it.

Embrace ambiguity and you will go far. Living in China teaches you to be comfortable with not knowing. It's not only the foreigners who don't know what's going on. The Chinese people don't know either. Everything is changing too quickly.

CALL HOME

You probably don't need me to tell you, but calling your friends and family back home is also a good way to combat culture shock and homesickness. Although you may have many good Chinese friends, speaking with them is not the same as speaking with someone from your home country. You will be able to vent a little to them, but don't expect them to understand what you are going through. They probably haven't had that type of experience to know what you are feeling.

I usually use Skype to call home since it is free from computer to computer and very cheap (2 US cents a minute) to call a cell phone.

DON'T COMPLAIN

If you haven't figured this out by now, you should. Complaining doesn't change anything, it brings others down and it drains a lot of energy. When I hear foreigners complaining to each other in China, I typically stay away. If my closest foreign friends are complaining too much, I limit our interactions to hanging out only once or twice a week. People whining and complaining around you will kill your mood.

Complaining is definitely warranted sometimes and you should feel free to complain to your close foreign or Chinese friends when it's really needed, but don't make a habit of it. Complaining about China with fellow expats may be an easy way to bond, but the cost is high.

WATCH OR READ YOUR HOME COUNTRY'S NEWS

Watching or reading your home country's news is probably not something you would immediately think of when you are experiencing heavy culture shock or homesickness. However, it is one of the best techniques.

Hearing about what the Republicans are doing to attack the Democrats or what the Democrats are doing to the Republicans for five minutes is usually enough for me to feel excellent relative to my present circumstance in China. Watching a car commercial or hearing about a reality TV show will also help.

Reading stories about life back home or even hearing how slow life is in comparison with China will make me feel much better about being in China. Even dropping an email to a friend for news of home and hearing that nothing very exciting is going on makes me happy. I know I am not missing out and that my present situation is okay.

You are trying to experience what life back home is like without being there. For me, the news and talking to people always helped me remember how mundane and routine life back home usually was in comparison with life in China. Learning about life back home will put everything back into perspective, and you probably won't feel homesick for very long.

RETURN TO YOUR HOME COUNTRY ONCE PER YEAR

Returning to your home country once a year will keep life in China fresh. From time to time you might feel that you are missing out on life back home, but I assure you, at least if you live in the United States, not that much is changing. Leaving China for a while will keep it interesting, and when you come back you will be reenergized. After being in China for a year or two without leaving you will probably have the feeling of "I need to get out of here!", and leaving for a month or two before returning will be a good thing. Going to Hong Kong for a mini retreat to escape the craziness from time to time is also a good idea.

MAKE FOREIGN FRIENDS

Many people out there may groan when they think about moving to China and then hanging out with other expats. While I can understand this sentiment and certainly spend much more time with Chinese friends overall than I do my fellow expat brothers and sisters, living in a country as different as China, with its cultural and linguistic differences, definitely necessitates having a support group of other foreigners you can rely on who can empathize with you when you are having a rough day.

Your foreign friends will be some of your best companions on your journey in China. The best year I experienced in China was because I had two foreign friends who were down to earth that I could hang out with on a regular basis. None of us complained too much, and when we needed someone to talk to we had each other for support.

You don't need to be best friends with the foreigners you hang out with, but it's generally a good thing to have someone to talk to and hang out with who is also having their own "China experience."

In general, foreigners can be found in the nicer places

around the city: Starbucks, Burger King, authentic foreign restaurants, foreign bars, Chinese language schools, hostels, universities, English training centers. There are generally foreigners about in any first, second, or third tier cities. The only time you may be out of luck is if the city is smaller than these and there isn't anything foreign there. Below is a list of where to meet other foreigners in China.

Starbucks

A city's foreignness can also be measured by the number of Starbucks in the city. The ratio of Starbucks to foreigners is positively correlated and linear though the exact ratio is still unknown. You can usually spot a foreigner or two at any given time at Starbucks. The staff can also usually speak English and might also have ideas on where foreigners hang out in the city.

University Campuses

If you are new to the city, it might be a good idea to have a local friend tell you where different universities can be found. If you are teaching, at least a few of your students may even know some foreigners they can introduce to you.

Otherwise, if you simply hang around a university or college campus you will probably spot a foreigner eventually. As he or she is likely in the same boat you, in addition to being a friend, they would be a valuable source of information as to where in the city you might be able to meet other foreigners.

Foreign Bars

Foreign bars are a surefire way of meeting a lot of interesting people from all over the world.

"I said my goodbyes to my family when I first came to China, telling them I'd be back in a year. I've now lived here eleven years," a Canadian I met one of my first weeks in China told me while at Friend's Club, a foreign bar that's been in Zhongshan almost as long.

"As a kid, I traveled around the Sahara desert for ten years making three circuits in total," I overheard a Moroccan telling a colleague of mine at a bar.

If you want to meet a lot of people with interesting back stories you can find them here.

Authentic Foreign Restaurants

Because they are rare in many cities, foreigners will flock to authentic foreign restaurants. Restaurants such as these are usually Italian or Mexican; a good Indian restaurant will also attract many foreigners and is my favorite choice for where to eat in Zhongshan and whenever possible.

A note on finding authentic foreign restaurants: many restaurants claim to be "Western" and this is usually a sign that it is a Chinese-style restaurant, which usually does not have any authentic foreign food. A duped foreigner (we've all been there) might be hanging about hoping for something Western at such an establishment so you might be able to find one at these types of places.

Nice Hotels

The swankiest hotel in the city may have some foreigners, but even if it does they are likely there on business and know less about the city than you do. Thus, they may not be the best person to ask about the city, though they still could be good for blowing off steam or sharing a drink if that's what you need at the moment.

Chinese Language Schools

Chinese language schools are a great place to meet other foreigners since they are the sole clients of such establishments. Furthermore, if you are studying Chinese at a place like this you would have that in common with the other foreigners and therefore could make friends without needing to randomly approach them in a bar or restaurant.

Chinese language schools, along with bars and hostels, also usually put on different types of events (especially during Western holidays), where many foreigners will socialize together.

Hostels
The majority of cities in China will not have a hostel in them, but if you are living in a tourist city such as Beijing or somewhere like Hangzhou or Yangshuo, there will be lots of opportunities to meet backpackers and travelers of all kinds at hostels.

Resources for Finding Other Foreigners
Below are a few social networking websites that will also be valuable for making foreign friends.

- **Guangzhou Stuff** (www.gzstuff.com)
  A website designed to help English speakers in and around Guangzhou meet each other.

- **Shanghai Stuff** (www.shanghaistuff.com)
  A website designed to help English speakers in and around Shanghai meet each other.

- **Beijing Stuff** (www.bjstuff.com)
  A website designed to help English speakers in and around Beijing meet each other.

- **The Beijinger** (www.thebeijinger.com)
  A website for foreigners containing everything you might like to know about Beijing. There are travel and restaurant recommendations, classifieds, and more.

- **Shanghaiist** (www.shanghaiist.com)
  This is a China news website which caters to foreigners.

■ **Shanghai Expat** (www.shanghaiexpat.com)
This is a forum for foreigners living in and around Shanghai.

■ **EChina Cities** (www.echinacities.com)
This website has everything from articles on how to do something such as find an international school for your kids to city profiles.

■ **Lost Laowai** (www.lostlaowai.com)
This is a website offering advice to expats living in China.

CHAPTER 16

TURNING CHINA
INTO A CAREER

MORE MONEY, LESS DEBT

STARING AT MY BANK account, it was hard to believe what I was seeing. I had over $15,000 in the account, enough to pay off the remainder of my college student loans. I went to the website where I was to pay my loans. Like many young Americans straddled with student loan debt, I usually didn't make enough money in a month to pay off more than the minimum amount, which in my case had been a measly $250. But with the money from my last paycheck from my employer, an international manufacturer of retail displays, I now had enough to finally be rid of my debt at the age of twenty-eight. I logged on to the student loan website and instead of paying the usually $250, I paid off the remainder of the loan. It felt like ten thousand pounds had just been lifted off my shoulders.

I had only been working at my current company a year and a half, and thanks to the low cost of living in China, coupled with a job that pays United States wages, even a very modest income by United States standards, I was able to save quite a lot of money very quickly. Not only was I able to save enough to pay back debts, travel, and save, but I also had a very interesting job as an interpreter, translator, and English teacher at an international company.

I spent my days at our factory on the outskirts of Jiaxing, a medium-sized city of 4.5 million people outside of Shanghai. My days were now spent visiting suppliers and interpreting for foreign visitors who came to inspect the factories, helping my Chinese colleagues with their English, resolving communication issues, translating engineering documents, and occasionally helping out on the assembly line or flying some prototypes back home for client approval.

My evenings were spent hanging out with friends and colleagues, exploring Jiaxing, Hangzhou, Shanghai, Ningbo, or Suzhou on weekends, and generally basking in the equivalent of a $75,000 job back home.

After paying off my loans, I had to head out. I was taking a road trip with some friends to nearby Anhui province to go hiking in the mountains. I had gotten my license a month before, and my favorite activity in China, after speaking Chinese with locals, was driving around the Chinese countryside. After picking up the car near one of the city centers, close to where I lived, I drove to pick up my friends at their respective apartment buildings.

"Hey Nick, thanks for picking me up," my friend Bill said to me getting into the passenger seat. Bill worked for a Spanish company in Jiaxing and after meeting at a bar one night though a mutual friend, we became good friends.

"Do you have everything?" I asked.

"Yes, let's go!" he said.

After picking up two more foreigner friends we headed for the interstate and Anhui beyond.

In the next section, I will explain how to take your China experience to the next level. I talk mainly about how to find a job at a company and what other opportunities there are for working in China.

CHAPTER 17

FINDING A JOB
IN CHINA

THE LINKEDIN METHOD
FOR FINDING A JOB

"IF YOU WANT THE job, it's yours," my future boss told me over the phone.

After four years of applying to non-teaching jobs in the United States and four years after my college graduation, I had my first full time US salary job. And it was in China.

The Job Search

I'd spent the last several years teaching English in China, and despite the cushy life it afforded, I didn't plan to be an English teacher forever. The ideal job, I had always thought, would be to work at a company that works with China and be sent to China with a US salary.

Like many college graduates in the United States who graduated around 2007, I'd had little luck finding jobs on Indeed, Craigslist, and Monster. Aside from the auto-generated email once a position had been filled six months later, I would very rarely hear back about a job. In all those years, I had two phone interviews, and screwed up another interview because I'd told the interviewer that my dream was to have my own business one day and she therefore saw me as the competition.

Because my success rate was so low, I decided I needed a change in tactics. One day, I suppose because I had failed to get a job for so many years, I suddenly got smarter about the whole process. I realized that many positions are probably not advertised and that I had a much better chance of getting a job if I knew someone who was looking to hire an individual like me. That meant that if I could just find the right person, who happened to be looking to hire someone with my skill set in the near future, I'd have a better chance of being hired than applying to online job postings for positions that probably eventually get filled by someone with better connections anyway or are not paid much attention to.

How to "Apply" for a Job
"You seem like a really cool dude, Nick."

I was making great progress. The vice president of sales at a successful international business that had offices in three countries, including China, had referred to me as a "cool dude" near the end of our 30-minute Skype conversation.

"Do you know what you'd even do here?" he asked me, referring to how I would help their company. Under normal circumstances, a phrase like this would frighten me, but judging from his tone of voice, he was actually thinking of ways I could help their company because he thought I would be a valuable asset.

Never apply to a job again. You will find the job you want much, much faster doing it the way I now do it. The following section is about how to secure a job in China using LinkedIn. There are many other ways you could secure a job without LinkedIn or in your home country so pay attention to the principals.

Finding a Job Using LinkedIn

Companies want to hire you.

That is, the *right* companies want to hire you. The beauty of LinkedIn is that it allows you to connect with the people in these right companies that want to hire you. Once they connect with you and you charm the heck out of them, they will probably want to hire you, even if they do not have the perfect job in mind for you yet. Many small and medium-sized companies are hiring lots of people, and once you are on their radar, you will be one of the next people picked for an interview.

The first step is finding the right type of company.

Think about your skill set and what type of company you want to work for. Think about the types of companies that would want to hire you. For me, this was a foreign company that had a presence in China. I wanted to be their "China Conduit": someone who got along well with the people and was able to bridge the cultural and linguistic gap. The important thing here is to think about what skills you have to offer a company.

Search by company on LinkedIn using a keyword (I used the word "China") to find companies related to what you have in mind and filter by size of company. I like to look at smaller companies of 200 people or less because they probably do not have the bureaucracy of larger companies and would be more flexible in the types of positions that they create. This doesn't mean that this tactic won't work for larger companies. Once you find a company, read their profile and take a look at their website to confirm that they actually do something you think would be interesting or that would fit you.

Now look at all of the employees of that company on LinkedIn and look for someone who would be able to do the hiring: a director of some kind, a human resources person, a CEO, or owner are all good choices. Try to find their personal email address on their profile page near the bottom. If you cannot find it, you can send them a message on LinkedIn but you will need to pay for this service. Otherwise you can also look for an email address on the company website to send it to. Look for an info, HR, or marketing email address. The initial email addresses I used to find two jobs I was ultimately hired for were both info email addresses.

Send a short message to the person or company telling them how you could help. Focus on their needs but let them know all about you at the same time. Here is the message I sent back in 2011:

> To Whom it May Concern,
>
> Hi my name is Nick Lenczewski, and I found out about <Company Name> through LinkedIn. I have been living in southern China's Guangdong province for four years. I've spent the majority of my time teaching English to students of all ages and recently started an English training center with my business partner. I speak Chinese proficiently, can read and write, and have HSK (a Chinese certification) certification. My background is in mathematics.
>
> I am returning to the US in hopes of finding a job at a company that deals with China on a regular basis, and was hoping my experience and talents could be of use at <Company Name>.
>
> Please let me know if you have such a need. I attached my resume for your convenience.
>
> Sincerely,
> Nick Lenczewski

You are not "applying" to any job. You are instead making contact with an actual person (we don't want machines as you will likely never hear back) in hopes of creating a real connection. Maybe they have a job for you, maybe they don't, maybe they will make up a job for you, but in my experience if you do this right you will at least hear back from your target fifty percent of the time or more.

The simple act of sending a message will make a big impression as very few people do this. I've done some recruiting in the past and been astounded by the number of applications where people did not even bother to write my name even though it was on the page they were using to apply. This may not seem important, but when you are looking at dozens of applications and there is one that's made an attempt at personalization, it will stick out more than the rest. Make a good impression and keep your message short. You can also attach a resume if you like, but the message is the important part here.

Get Hired
The first time I used this tactic I spent an hour and sent out about five emails in one night. I heard back from one company the next day, and they ultimately hired me six weeks later.

The second time I used this tactic I sent out ten to twenty such emails over the course of a week, heard back from seventy percent of them, and one eventually lead to an interview and job six months later when a position opened up.

It's not a great feeling when you scour the internet for some semblance of the type of job you are looking for only to find one after three hours of searching, apply, and be fairly sure it was never read by anyone. The process I use eliminates a lot of this pain.

Before anyone starts to say, "Well you were lucky because you can speak Mandarin that's really valuable!" let me emphasize that I'd applied to many jobs with Mandarin on my resume and in my cover letters. The same goes for my mathematics degree. In my experience, companies aren't interested in majors or that you can learn on the job. They are looking for people who can do the work they need done as soon as possible. They are looking for applicable skills and experience, not knowledge. If you can show the right person that you know what they're doing, you know how to help them, are easy to get along with, and are reliable, you're eighty percent of the way towards landing a job.

You may not be able to speak great Mandarin just yet, and maybe you've never lived in China before, but I guarantee there are people with no Mandarin or China experience that have landed good jobs in China. The important part is to use the principles outlined above and the tools at your disposal to land your ideal position in China (or anywhere for that matter).

Traits Foreign Companies In China Look For

Your most important asset when looking for a non-teaching job in China is not your language skills or your cultural understanding. While these things definitely help, the most important thing foreign companies look for is a core competency. You need a core competency to find a non-teaching job in China. This could be something related to finance, trade, manufacturing, engineering, management, or computer programming among many others, depending on the company. After you have this core competency, an employer will also consider your linguistic and cultural understanding capabilities, but these are not as important as the skill of doing the work that needs to be done.

INTERVIEWING

"Hi Nick, I spoke with the hiring manager about you and he would like to interview you. Can you come in for an interview?" This was the recruiter from Nstarts Consulting, a recruiting company I had made contact with online in order to see what types of non-teaching jobs I could get in China.

A few days later, I took the bus from Zhongshan, where I was living at the time, to Shenzhen, a few hours away. I found the office of the company I was to interview at in Shekou, a district filled with expats and foreign companies. Amidst the balmy heat and palm trees, I made my way to the office.

Research the Company and Employees

Many people get nervous before interviews and I am no different. However, over the years I have gotten better at them and learned a few things on how to make a great impression without being a fruitcake. I want to share these tips with you below.

Before you step into the room, you will need to do some research about the company and the people there such as your interviewer, your future boss, and your future colleagues. Go onto the company's website and make sure you know what they do. Look at their About Us page, their Company History and Background pages, and where they are located worldwide. Try to find the company in the news and read about current projects and new products. Read the LinkedIn profiles of people at the company or those who have held a similar position to the one you are applying for. Try to get as good a feel for the company and the position as possible.

Ask Good Questions

"So you are interpreter?" my would-be boss asked me in the interview.

"Yes, that was part of my role at my last company," I replied.

"But what you know about business? Seems like you don't have a lot of experience in the foreign trade. Mostly you are a teacher," he said.

It can be difficult to get an interview at a company where there is no component from your last job involved. But by showing your interviewer you're adept in more than one area, and by not being like other interviewees that just sit there and answer questions like a robot (I've interviewed lots of people like this), you'll be able to stand out.

If you are unfamiliar with how companies in general operate and what different positions might entail (as I was until about age twenty-five), I recommend checking out The Personal MBA (www.personalmba.com). You can read all about how companies are formed, why, and what the critical elements of a business or company are.

In my case, the position I had applied to was a sales and marketing position. "Actually I used to run an English school. It involved marketing and selling, getting parents of students interested in our classes and teachers. I'm also very good with people," I said. I pulled as much information as possible from my previous experiences and then started to ask him some of my own questions.

How big is your company? How many people are there? Who are the other people in my department in similar positions and what are their backgrounds? How has the company been doing recently? What big problems have you had? This is how I think that I could help, what do you think? Ask as many of these types of questions as possible and always be thinking, "How can I be the answer to this person's prayers?"

"Well, I don't know. It just seems like you don't have any experience," he continued. Sometimes despite all your best efforts, it is still difficult to convince some people that you have what it takes, even though it may seem obvious to you and your friends.

"*Ng hai, ngaw yiu ging yan.*" For some reason I started speaking to him in Cantonese. No, I have experience, I told him. The look in my would-be boss's eyes changed and he looked at me like I would now able to do the job.

"So, you can speak some Cantonese too?"

Why he cared that I could speak a little Cantonese when I had been a Mandarin interpreter for almost two years, I didn't know. "Many of our clients speak Cantonese and they would be very impressed. Thank you for coming in, Nick, you will hear from us with an offer soon."

In the last few moments, I had impressed this man enough for him to want to hire me with some feeble Cantonese. You never know what will happen or how and why you might be hired, so keep at it.

As a foreigner in China it's not difficult to find non-teaching work if you're looking in the right places and out there hustling. Regardless of whether you get a job or not, you will gain some valuable experience.

RESOURCES

■ **LinkedIn** (www.linkedin.com)
This is the best job-finding tool out there. However, do not waste time trying to apply for jobs. Instead, you should look for *companies* that would hire someone like you to do a job, and find one of the owners or employees who knows of current or upcoming openings and contact them.

■ **Nstarts** (www.nstarts.com)
This is a recruiting company I've used to land a job interview. At my previous company in China, we also used this site to find people for positions. They cater specifically to expats.

■ **Delta Bridges** (www.deltabridges.com)
This is an online forum for expats living in Guangdong province and has a job board. There are many such websites out there and as you know, I'm opposed to the idea of

wasting time applying to jobs. But I have a friend who did find a job as a chemist in Shenzhen using this site.

■ **China Jobs** (www.chinajobs.com)
This website is the largest online job posting website for foreigners seeking employment in China I have seen. Most positions are English teaching positions, but there are also some non-teaching postings.

■ **Atlas China** (www.atlas-china.com)
This website is strictly for foreigners who can speak Mandarin and for companies that are seeking Mandarin-speaking foreigners. You create a video of yourself speaking Mandarin and put it online for employers to see.

CHAPTER 18

WORKING AT A COMPANY IN CHINA

*"Choose a job you love, and you will never have
to work a day in your life."*
—CONFUCIUS

THE LIFE OF A CULTURAL LIAISON

I BIKED IN TO work on a beautiful spring day in 2012 after sipping my overpriced $6 small *xiangcao natie* (vanilla latte) at a Starbucks below my apartment in Jiaxing, a medium-sized city of 4.5 million people, an hour and a half outside of Shanghai. I worked at a nearby factory as a cultural liaison and would bike the two miles to work every day through the streets lined with factories, which churned out everything from rakes to car batteries for the entire world.

I had never imagined that such a job as cultural liaison

existed, but apparently it did because I was doing it. It may have also been in part thanks to my background and what I wanted to do so that a position as ideal as this one was created for me.

The company office had a dozen green and grey cubicles in a carpeted area of a factory where my three dozen Chinese, American, and New Zealand colleagues, mainly product managers, engineers, buyers, and I worked alongside one another.

In my role as cultural liaison, I was responsible for everything language and culture related. The root of many companies' problems is bad communications. Besides managers, departments don't speak with one another or people's ideas are not heard and never implemented even when they would actually save time and money. Add to this a company that needs to navigate two very different cultures and languages, and the need for a cultural liaison becomes apparent.

After teaching an hour of English each morning, talking about everything from US retail, to types of screws, to powder coated metal, I'd settle down at my desk to peruse LinkedIn for potential hires. My boss wanted me to find project managers and engineers who had experience abroad and had worked with big American retail clients like Target, Wal-Mart, or Best Buy. I had some good luck with LinkedIn and found dozens of candidates over the 18 months at the company, and a few that were eventually hired on, including one key manager.

In the afternoons, our company driver, our secretary and I might go out looking for potential suppliers for our company. The goal was to build a list of pre-qualified suppliers that our buyers would be able to rely on when purchasing retail display parts.

"*Nimen shi waiqi laide, shi ma?*" You are from a foreign enterprise, correct? The head of sales at the factory greeted us at the entrance before showing us around his factory, which made printed circuit boards.

Late that afternoon, back at the office, I'd help one of my fellow foreign colleagues communicate with our prototyping team. They'd been working on an interactive display for a customer. The welder knew how to weld and my colleague knew just about everything about how to build anything, but neither spoke the other's language and it was a common occurrence for me to be in the middle of such discussions about how best to fabricate something, with both Chinese and Western ways of thinking thrown in.

"Our customer in the US will like it like this way."

"But in China we make things like this."

"We can make it this way once, but producing ten thousand of these with the same precision will be difficult."

Such was my work life in Jiaxing at an international manufacturer of custom retail displays.

This Man Is Too Dark
"So, what do you think?" asked a printing supplier.

"It looks great. Thank you." My boss, an American, was admiring some graphics that had been outsourced to a printing company. However, the printing company boss still looked troubled.

"Don't you think the man is too dark? I mean it's difficult to see him."

My boss looked perplexed, he could see the man in the advertisement just fine.

"I think we should lighten him up so people can see him," the Chinese boss continued.

Finally it dawned on my boss, the man didn't realize that the man in the artwork was black.

You had to love working in China at times like this and fortunately there are many such humorous misunderstandings. Every foreigner in China has at least a handful of these types of stories and they are just one of the pieces that make China such an interesting place to be at this time in history.

Although these stories are entertaining, there are definitely other miscommunications, which can be a danger when doing business here. Such issues can cause lots of headaches, and cost lots of time and money. Thus, there is the need for the cultural liaison in China, where East and West meet, and bad grammar and manners start to cause trouble. It's easy to attribute all miscommunication in general, to either a barrier of language or of culture. However, it is important to make the distinction between the two. Language barrier problems are relatively easy to solve most of the time. Even if one can't speak the language, language problems can usually be solved with an electronic dictionary, correct grammar in writing, pictures, drawings, pointing, an interpreter or translator. Cultural miscommunication is where the trouble usually lies.

The Cultural Gap

"You say we need to make the bracket tighter. I think it is already very tight, but we can do that," said my Chinese colleague over the phone to our American colleague in the US.

"No, the bracket is too tight," he said.

"I know, it's not a problem."

Thankfully, I was sitting next to my Chinese colleague who, because of a grammatical error, misunderstood the email from her Western colleague. My American colleague had left off an "o" in the phrase "too tight," and I knew my Chinese colleague, because of her sound understanding of English grammar and spelling, had assumed "to tight" meant something like "to tighten." Unfortunately she lacked the cultural insight us Americans often take for granted in these cultural mashups, as most of us would understand what my American colleague meant when he wrote "to tight." This is why my Chinese colleague thought that a particular bracket needed to be tighter in order to receive the okay from a big US retailer we were trying to please, so that we could start mass production and meet our shipping window when it was the opposite that was true.

At other times, an American colleague might explain something to a Chinese colleague but use too many colloquialisms that even a bilingual Chinese person would not know.

"Get 'er done."

"Take a rain check."

"Dime a dozen."

While it would be valuable for my Chinese colleagues to learn such phrases, which they all eventually did, it usually prompted more work than necessary in order to understand what someone meant when dropping such idioms in conversation for the first time.

In companies where instructions can change daily and the input of engineers who can't speak much English is valuable, someone with a lot of empathy and the ability to understand both parties is a valuable asset to any organization in China where Westerners and Chinese are working together. The ability to translate documents and interpret in meetings or on factory visits is also very valuable and will only make you more marketable for a job in China.

RESOURCES

Below are resources that will help any foreign company in China dealing with language and culture related problems. Whether you are doing business in China, teaching in China, or traveling, the below resources will help you understand the Chinese culture better, and also help you understand your own better.

■ **China Mike** (www.china-mike.com)

Check the Culture & Society section for good articles about China's culture and how this affects daily life and work as a foreigner. Mike's other pages are also good sources for information on travel to some of the better known destinations in China.

■ **Poorly Made in China by Paul Midler**

"Why are my shampoo bottles so thin?! The samples weren't like this!" yells an irritated US businessman trying to source shampoo from China. Mr. Midler on the other end of the line, has heard this same type of thing dozens of times throughout his career in China.

Poorly Made in China is Paul's Midler's true-life experience working as a cultural and linguistic conduit between Chinese factories and Western companies, solving the cross-cultural troubles they are having with China while doing business. The clash of cultures, the ridiculous stories of quality degrading shipment by shipment, and Midler's observations make a great story. Almost anyone who has done business in or with China will have one or two of their own such stories and they are always worth a listen.

This book is also helpful if you are considering working at a manufacturing or trade company in China.

CHAPTER 19

FREELANCE TUTORING

TEACHING PRIVATE STUDENTS

MANY COLLEGES IN CHINA have a midday break that is two to three hours long. At Zhongshan College this break lasts from 11:40 a.m. to 2:30 p.m. In between, students and teachers usually have lunch and take a nap. At this time my fellow foreign English teachers and I would oftentimes have lunch at a nearby mall.

On one such occasion my Australian friend, Tom, and I had had lunch at a Japanese restaurant in the mall before relaxing with a cup of milk tea at a nearby cafe. As two o'clock approached, we started to head back up the hill to the college to teach our afternoon classes. The mall was not large, but did make for a good maze if it was your first or second time there. The shops were always changing too, shop owners going in and out of business rapidly.

"Hi, sir? Hi!" a woman was yelling to us from behind. We stopped to wait for her to catch up. "I've been looking all over for you two. I saw you come into the mall but couldn't find you," she explained.

As a foreigner in China, you tend to stick out a lot and this was not the first time we'd been singled out from the crowd for how we looked. We waited to hear what the woman had to say.

"This is my business card for my English school," she said, giving us cards. "I just opened an English Training Center near here and we are looking for foreign English teachers. If you want to teach class at my school you can contact me."

We thanked her for her offer and then we were on our way again. This wasn't the first time either of us had been approached to teach English outside of the college where we were employed, but it was the first time I was contacted three times in the same day with offers to teach English. Later that day I was asked to teach a friend of a friend's child, and was also asked by a student of mine if I could tutor his cousin.

Foreign English Teachers Are in Demand

Most expats that live in China will discover that the demand for learning English is huge. There are new English training centers opening up all the time. Foreign brands and products are symbols of wealth that many people strive to obtain. Many Chinese also realize that the education system in United States, Australia, or Canada is better than the Chinese education system and if they have enough money, they want to send their kids abroad for school. In order to go abroad, the students need to pass a number of tests in English, such as the TOEFL or IELTS. In addition to passing these tests, parents want their kids to be ready to interact effectively with the outside world. One of the main ways to address these challenges is to find a foreign English teacher for their children. As most of the world is aware by now, the new rich in China are growing rapidly and thus the demand for a private foreign English teacher is always on the rise. You could be one of these foreign English teachers.

Tutoring Students in English

Shirley was a 14-year-old girl preparing to go to high school in Australia. Her mother had hired me to teach English in several different subject areas including biology, math, and chemistry for 200 RMB an hour ($30/hr.). Shirley and her mother would come to my apartment twice a week on afternoons when I didn't have class and we would talk and learn for an hour and a half.

Classes went smoothly as Shirley was bright and she and her mother were respectful and kind. I enjoyed teaching her and students like her because they were very inquisitive, and we didn't need to stop for any other students since it was just her. The pay was great for China and I also charged my other private students the same 200 RMB hourly rate.

I met Shirley through one of my students at the college where I taught. My student had told me his cousin was looking for an English teacher and asked if I was interested in meeting his cousin, who turned out to be Shirley.

"Thank you for class today, Nick," said Shirley's mother after we finished class. "One of my friends is also looking for an English teacher, would you be able to meet with her sometime?"

Through Shirley and her mother, I found another student, and it went like this until I had four different students I was meeting with once or twice a week.

Some of these students came to my apartment, other times I would go to their apartment. I taught one set of students in a restaurant their parents owned, and another pair of students in an office of a garment factory their parents owned. Some students needed me to help them prepare for classes abroad and we studied for the IELTS examination, other students were there because their parents wanted them to be better at oral English, and so we did a lot of similar work to what my college students did. One of my students was a professional pianist, another student of mine was three years old, but most of my students were primary school, middle school, or high school age.

There are all types of people in China looking to improve their English and many of them will pay you well for it. When I taught English lessons, it was mostly supplemental work in addition to my teaching English at a college. However, I have heard stories of foreigners making this type of teaching their sole job in China. They build a large network of students, mainly through word of mouth, teach up to five students at the same time, and charge them each 100 RMB, which comes out to about $80 per hour.

Finding Private Students
As with any type of freelance work, word of mouth and referrals are the key. In order to find private students, talk with your college students, and ask them if they know anyone.

After you find students, try to teach them for an hour and a half to two hours at a time so that you get paid more for your time. If you can get 10 hours of work per week at $30 per hour, that amounts to $300 per week, which is already $1200 per month. From there, increase the number of hours you work, and try to get multiple students in one class in order to raise rates up to $50 or $80 per hour. At $80 per hour, working 20 hours per week is $6,400 a month, and more than $75,000 per year.

Instead of trying to directly make freelance tutoring your sole income, you could first find a full time job at a college or training center. Start out by teaching students privately on the side until you have enough students to make it a full time job.

CHAPTER 20

DRIVING IN CHINA

GETTING A CHINESE DRIVER'S LICENSE

"WOMEN JINTIAN HAO XIANG you yi ge waiguoren kaoshi." It looks like we have a foreigner taking the test today.

The DMV test administrator was speaking to a crowd of Chinese people and me, who were lined up at the Jiaxing DMV to take our written driver's license examination. *"Guo lai."* Come over here. The administrator said, looking and gesturing towards me to come to the front of the line. Being a foreigner in China could be so sweet sometimes.

The Written Exam

I'd been studying to take the written driver's examination for the last few months. I had studied all 1,500 possible questions, taken many practice exams, and now felt ready for the test. I had to get a 90 percent and answer all 100 questions within an hour. The time limit would be no problem, but many of the questions were not intuitive and bad translations of easy questions create wrong answers instantly.

I was the first person to enter the testing area and was seated at a computer to take the exam. Foreigners wishing to get their Chinese driver's license must have their native driver's license translated into Chinese by a designated translation agency, go through a number of medical tests and checks, pay a small fee, and pass a written examination (no road test required). In my opinion, the biggest pain was getting all of the documents in order, because if anything is even a little off, you will be told to go back to the hospital or go get your license translated by a different company.

The exam went pretty well and I felt like I was doing a great job. There were a few tough questions though and I started to worry that I had gotten more than ten wrong. That was alright though, the rules said everyone got to take the exam a second time immediately after the first if they did not pass.

I answered the final question and my final score popped up: 89. *Cao.* Damn. I got up to see the administrator about taking the test again.

"*Wai guo ren zhi neng kao yi ci,*" he said. Foreigners can only take the test once.

You're kidding me. I was going to have to come back a week later in order to take the test again. In China, you will learn that you can never be sure of anything ever no matter what anyone says, until it is actually happening, and even then, you must be prepared for it to radically change at any moment. Many foreigners who live long term in China learn to adopt this mindset. The Chinese also have this mindset since life in their country is so unpredictable.

I went back to the DMV the next week and was able to pass. For more on getting the correct study materials and learning where to take the exam see the resources at the end of this section.

SELDOM FOLLOWED RULES OF THE ROAD

As a driver on the road, you will quickly learn that many of the rules from the driving exam are not followed, and if you do try to follow them, you will cause an accident. Try not to get angry when people cut you off since it will happen every time you drive.

Instead of getting angry, realize that there is indeed a flow and there are rules that people do follow. Put aside the fact that you will witness some terrible driving, and instead embrace the flow. Be like water. Remember learning about looking both ways before crossing a street when you were a kid? I'm not sure everyone has learned this in China, so make sure you don't hit any of these non-lookers as you cruise the streets.

Tolls and Interstates

Interstates in China require tolls. They are not cheap either. The plus side is that many of them have very few cars because of these tolls. Although you will need to pay 150 RMB for your three-hour ride, you will be one of the only cars on the road.

The interstates are very sophisticated and you can get all the way from Hong Kong to Kazakhstan by following them. There are attendants at every tollgate so exact change is not necessary.

Cameras and Fines

"Slow down up ahead, there's a camera," my friend and passenger, Bill said.

In the United States, we have state patrols driving around with speed guns looking for speeders and when they find someone who is at least ten miles over the speed limit, they pull them over and possibly give them a ticket. In China, there are too many people for this to be an effective system. Instead, there are thousands of cameras set up all over China's highways that measure the speed of cars and take a picture of the car's license plate if it is driving too fast. A few days later, this person receives a ticket in the mail. They can also tell if you're going the wrong way down a one way and will also fine you for this. I was fined once for this. Everyone else was doing it.

I slowed down as we passed under a camera. Looking down at my phone to use Google Maps, I made sure we were still on the right track.

"Twenty meters ahead another camera," Bill said again.

"How do you know?" I asked.

He showed me the map on his phone. "Baidu Maps."

Baidu is the Google of China, and a very innovative company when it comes to maps and driving.

Renting a Car

While you may not want to buy a car in China, though you certainly can, a great option is renting a car. Cars are cheap to rent in China and will only set you back 100-200 RMB ($15-$30) per day. Many cities have an eHi Car Service, which is what I use every time I rent a car.

RESOURCES

Arguably my favorite type of instant adventure in China is taking a road trip. To do this legally you'll need a Chinese Driver's License and a car. Licenses are good for 6 years.

■ **Chinese Driving Test** (www.chinese-driving-test. com)

Take practice exams and study questions from the exam. Some of the translations were not very good in 2012 when I took the exam so hopefully things have improved. You can only take the English version once per visit. If you do not get a ninety percent, you will need to come back a week later to take it again.

■ **eHi Car Services** (http://en.1hai.cn)

This car rental service has outlets all over China. Booking a car is actually very easy and can be done over the phone, even in English. You may need to go to a physical location first to set up your account with your phone number, but afterwards renting a car should not be difficult. Bring a passport and both flaps of your Chinese Driver's License.

CHAPTER 21

STARTING A BUSINESS

DOING BUSINESS IN CHINA

"EVERY PERSON I KNEW who went off to China thinking they'd strike it rich came home with a chopstick up his ass."

My friend said this to me when I told him of my own plans to start a business in China. He was the most successful person I knew back home and had decades of experience working in the Far East. This wasn't helping my cause, but it didn't stop me from going to China and starting an English training center anyway. However, in retrospect, I can see how what he was saying was true. I too came home in the end with no more money than when I had started (though not less either).

Starting a business anywhere is going to necessitate some risk taking. I don't believe that starting a successful business in China is any more difficult than in any part of the world, but starting one in China does have its own quirks, which can work against you or in your favor.

As a foreigner, you will be discriminated against in the business arena and this is just how it is. Typically, foreigners will need more money than their Chinese counterparts to start a business, and there are stricter requirements. Most enterprises started by a foreigner will need to have a Chinese partner. If the partner is good, you're in luck. If the partner is not who you thought they were, it could be a nightmare.

There will be a lot of red tape to go through as well. When my friends and I started an English training center, we had to consult with many different bureaus in the city to make sure we were meeting all of the requirements so that we would have a legitimate business. Our school needed to have at least six classrooms, plenty of windows, enough chairs and desks, and more. It was only then that we would be granted a business license for the particular type of school we were running.

Types of Businesses

Everything you do will depend on the type of business you start. This is very important to realize, as some businesses will probably be easier to start than others. For example if you are starting a factory that produces motorbikes for the Chinese market, this will take a lot more time and resources than importing chips or diapers. If you are selling something to the Chinese market, there will be different requirements than if you are making something in China and selling it to a market outside of China.

I recommend speaking with other entrepreneurs who have started businesses in China and see what they have to say. Compare all the different types of businesses and possibilities to see what's right for you. In addition, you should probably be living in China first before starting a business. Teaching English is good way to first come to China and get set up.

RESOURCES

If you're looking to do business in China, you can check out some of the websites and books below. As with many sites online it is difficult to discover how successful people are or aren't, but I believe the below sites offer some good advice.

■ **China Entrepreneur by Juan Antonio Fernandez and Laurie Underwood**
This book talks about what makes a successful entrepreneur in China. In it, they cover everything from how to hire the correct types of people to setting up the correct business entity. It's based on interviews with successful foreign entrepreneurs in China.

■ **The Elevator Life** (www.theelevatorlife.com)
A video blog made by two Americans living in China, designing brands and products sourced from China and selling their products to the world via online stores. They offer their advice on how to successfully navigate the Chinese business culture and interview other entrepreneurs in Asia. They also have an importing business importing wine into China. More and more Chinese consumers are buying wine.

■ **China Business Cast** (www.chinabusinesscast.com)
This website contains a series of podcasts of interviews with entrepreneurs in China. The advice they give paints a good picture of what one might be able to expect when launching a startup in China.

■ **Startup Noodle** (www.startupnoodle.com)
Startup Noodle is a blog offering advice to would-be entrepreneurs in China from a foreign entrepreneur in China himself. You may contact the owner with questions about startups in China.

■ **Tropical MBA** (www.tropicalmba.com)
A blog and podcast about location-independent businesses, many of which are in Asia. A location-independent

business is a business that can be operated from a laptop or phone with an Internet connection from anywhere around the world. Such businesses often include online stores, software development, writing, translating services, and graphic design. The website has a series of podcast episodes and most of their interviews are with other entrepreneurs in Asia, including China. Not many of the guests seem to be selling in China, but many of them source products from there. Worth a listen.

CHAPTER 22

EPILOGUE
Embracing Uncertainty

"Awe is what moves us forward."
—JOSEPH CAMPBELL, *Reflections on the Art of Living*

IF YOU'VE READ THIS far and you're still interested in going to China, and I hope you are, I recommend talking with someone who has worked in China. Chances are that someone you know knows someone who has taught English or worked in China. Looking at some of the different resources, films, and books mentioned in this guide will also give you some clearer ideas about whether you'd like to go or not. Taking a few Mandarin classes in your home country may also spark some further interest in going to China.

The main trait you will need to cultivate in order to live in China is that of embracing uncertainty. As I've mentioned several times in this guide already, the systems in

China for dispersing information are still relatively primitive. You won't know a lot about what is happening or what will happen until it is happening. At first, you may find this annoying, but after a while, if you learn to embrace it, it can be liberating. It will force you to live more in the moment, and as a result there will be more surprises, usually for the better. And even when the surprises are not for the better, it will teach you to be flexible and patient.

The Journey Home

The most difficult part of your adventure in China will be the journey home. Whether you are in China for one year or 20 years, chances are you that at some point you will have urges to return to the society you came from. If you do decide to return to where you came from one day, a true challenge lies in integrating your experience back into daily life there.

You will have experienced things that few people back home will be able to understand. You'll have had a major life-changing experience that you think everyone should experience. You'll tell people about it, and many of your friends will find it interesting and you may inspire them to go on their own adventure. Other people, though they may find it interesting, have their own lives to live, and your experience many not apply to their current situation. They will be happy to see you, but for many, adventure in foreign lands seldom enters their thoughts. As you try and talk to these people about your experience, you may even get discouraged.

Many strangers may see you as weird. "Did you live in a cave?" one dental hygienist asked me once when I told her I had lived in China. Lol. How others react to you reveals more about them than it does about you.

The journey home has been undertaken by millions of people throughout history. Some cannot do it and eventually return to the wild and continue to live in that other world for a long time. Others stay in their home country, but close themselves off from society, preferring to continue pursuit of their soul's calling in private. And then there are those who fight to integrate their experience into their home society.

This is the most difficult path. Maybe you will become a teacher, teaching others about the world you have experienced, and work on your art in your free time. Maybe you will start a company that people care about and you will change society for the better, spreading your message. Or maybe you will find new ways to continue to learn about China and help others to have the same life changing experiences you were blessed with.

ACKNOWLEDGMENTS

THANK YOU EVERYONE WHO read early drafts of this book and provided feedback: Mike Lenczewski, Jack Lenczewski, Nancy Markwardt, Mike Diliberto, Nels Erickson, Emma Chen, Corey Busch, John Kurth, Allen Huang, Wayne Lau, Harry He, and Ryan McCarthy.

Richard Bohr, thank you for your constant encouragement, your ideas for promoting the book, and belief in the book.

Joan Holman, thank you for your recommendations on how best to publish and market my book. Your advice and guidance has been invaluable.

Nels Erickson, thank you for all your support as I wrote this book and encouragement as I first started writing about my adventures in China on my blog.

Maryknoll Teach in China Service Project and Kevin Clancy, thank you for the opportunity to first come to China.

Paul Marsnik, thanks for the encouragement and listening when I've had China-related projects and business ideas I wanted to bounce off you.

Mike Diliberto, thank you for the opportunity to work as a cultural liaison in China.

Matt Callahan, thanks for guiding me as a young writer.

Richard LaBute, thank you for all the great stories of adventure in Asia and guidance over the years.

Thank you Tim Ferriss and James Altucher. Tim's book, *The Four Hour Workweek*, completely changed how I previously thought about work and partly inspired me to write this book. James's humorous writings on life and work have always been inspirational and spoken truth to me.

Thank you to the authors, artists, and entertainers who inspire me: Jerry Seinfeld, Sofia Coppola, Jess Row, Alan Watts, Joseph Campbell, Rick Steves, and JRR Tolkien.

Thank you to all of my friends in Zhongshan, Jiangmen, and Jiaxing, China. As the saying goes, the people make the place, and without all of the great people I've met in China I never would have stayed more than a year and none of this would have been worth writing about.

Thank you to Harry He and Dan Lei, your support relating to China matters is always appreciated whenever I am in Zhongshan, my home in Asia.

To my brothers, Jack and Mike Lenczewski, and my parents, Nancy and Joe Lenczewski. Thank you for all the love and humor, I love you all.

ABOUT THE AUTHOR

NICK LENCZEWSKI SPENT SIX years living in Guang-dong and Zhejiang provinces in China. During that time, he taught English at Zhongshan College in Guangdong province, became fluent in Mandarin Chinese, worked as a translator, interpreter, and cultural liaison for an international company in China, traveled to nine countries and twenty of China's provinces, made two 30-minute films, and perfected a job-finding tactic so that people of all ages would not need to worry about being unemployed for long amounts of time. He continues to find new ways to help promote understanding between China and the western world, and works as a Mandarin interpreter at his company, Chinese Interpreting Services, LLC (www.chineseinter-pretingservicesmn.com), which is based in Minneapolis, Minnesota.

You can contact him through his website, www.ultimat-echinaguide.com, and at nick@ultimatechinaguide.com. To see his most recent film, *Dreaming of Zhongshan*, go to: www.vimeo.com/129442903 or http://v.youku.com/v_show/id_XMTI1NjcxODYyNA if you are in China.

60153912R00124

Made in the USA
Charleston, SC
23 August 2016